FOREWORD

The primary objective of the OECD Nuclear Energy Agency (NEA) is to encourage co-operation among the governments in furthering the development of nuclear power as a safe, environmentally acceptable and economic energy source. In particular, the Nuclear Development Committee (NDC) of the NEA has the mandate to "ensure that appropriate technical and economic studies on nuclear energy development and the fuel cycle" are carried out.

Preparations are in hand in several countries for the disposal of highly radioactive waste and spent nuclear fuel, and there is a growing number of projects to decommission nuclear facilities such as nuclear power plants. There is increasing interest among policy makers and the general public in the financing of these activities. The NDC, therefore, decided to initiate a study on this topic to complement earlier work on the costs of nuclear electricity generation including waste management and disposal and decommissioning.

The main objectives of the study are to provide comprehensive information on policies established in Member countries for recognising and funding future financial liabilities arising from peaceful nuclear activities, to analyse how these policies meet the "polluter pays" principle and to ensure the sustainability of nuclear power programmes.

Experts from 12 NEA countries and two international organisations participated in the expert group convened by the NEA (see Annex 3). Information and data were collected through a questionnaire sent to NEA Member countries in 1994. Responses were received from 16 NEA countries.

This report is the result of collaborative efforts of experts in this field but it does not necessarily represent the views of participating countries or international organisations. It is published on the responsibility of the Secretary-General of OECD.

TABLE OF CONTENTS

EXECUTIVE SUMMARY

Introduction

In 1994, nuclear power plants contributed about 24 per cent of the electricity generation in NEA countries where some 340 nuclear units were in operation. The industry supporting nuclear power covers uranium mines, fuel cycle facilities and nuclear power plant construction and operation. Nuclear research is carried out in a number of centres and institutes. Radioisotopes are produced from nuclear reactors and laboratories and are widely used in research, medicine and industry. Nuclear research and industry makes a significant contribution to the technological, economic and social development in the world. All these activities, as it is the case in other industries, generate liabilities. Since the early days of peaceful application of nuclear energy, these liabilities have been recognised and mechanisms have been designed and implemented to cope with them.

Overall objectives and scope

This report deals with future financial liabilities arising from nuclear activities, in particular electricity generation, and with the mechanisms that NEA countries have put in place to ensure adequate funding of these liabilities when the need will occur.

In this report, future financial liabilities are defined as costs which an organisation or company is expected to meet in the future, i.e. beyond some five years, as a consequence of its current and past activities. Although the actual expenditures to discharge liabilities may lie far into the future, it has been recognised that consideration should be given to making provision now for funds to cover future expenditures.

The study provides a comprehensive picture on policies for recognising and funding future financial liabilities arising from nuclear activities and their implementation schemes in NEA Member countries. Mechanisms for reporting and funding future financial liabilities are described, analysed and compared. The report offers some findings, conclusions and recommendations for consideration by Member countries.

The nuclear activities considered in the report include nuclear R & D, nuclear industry sectors such as uranium mining and milling, conversion and enrichment, nuclear fuel fabrication, nuclear power plant operation and maintenance, and radioisotope production. Future financial liabilities arising from these activities cover management and disposal of radioactive waste, reprocessing of spent fuel when applicable, and decommissioning of facilities at the end of their life time.

A broad international consensus exists on the standards and code of practice regarding radioactive waste disposal. This consensus developed within the framework of international organisations such as the IAEA and NEA, goes even beyond financial liabilities and covers ethical issues. In this connection, the NEA Radioactive Waste Management Committee (RWMC) published in 1995 a collective opinion on the environmental and ethical basis of geological disposal of long-lived radioactive waste that addresses in particular inter-generation equity issues.

The present study addresses only liabilities arising from normal operations and excludes civil liabilities connected with nuclear accidents that are covered by international conventions on liability and compensation for nuclear damage.

Value of liabilities

The report is based upon information provided by NEA Member countries essentially in their responses to a questionnaire circulated by the Secretariat. Some countries, which did not answer the questionnaire, provided background information and data on the nuclear sector and liabilities. The data reflects the status as of mid-1994 when the information was collected. Country specific information on nuclear activities, estimated values of the liabilities and indicative scheduled timing of expenditures in connection with these liabilities, is summarised in Annex 1 of the report for those countries which provided data.

The absolute value of liabilities for radioactive waste disposal and decommissioning of nuclear power plants is estimated at several hundred million US dollars per unit. Previous NEA studies provide cost estimations for decommissioning of nuclear power plants and spent fuel disposal or reprocessing and high-level waste disposal. The discounted cost of decommissioning represents less than 1 per cent of the overall cost of a nuclear power plant. The costs of spent fuel disposal or reprocessing and high-level waste disposal amount to some 3 to 6 per cent of the overall nuclear electricity generation costs.

As shown in Annex 1, the timing of expenditures associated with discharging liabilities varies from country to country. The disbursement schedule depends mainly on: the country policy and regulations regarding the timing for dismantling and decommissioning nuclear facilities; the radioactive waste disposal option adopted e.g. near-surface site or deep geological formation; and the type of fuel cycle chosen, i.e., direct disposal of spent fuel or reprocessing.

Role of the State

The State is responsible for policy issues and the establishment of laws and regulations within which nuclear sector operators can fulfil their liabilities. In this connection, the State has generally acted to: ensure that future financial liabilities are recognised and taken into account by their generators as soon as they arise; assume responsibilities of "historic" waste whenever necessary; and, in some cases, establish as its responsibility the control and/or operation of activities generating nuclear liabilities.

The "Polluter Pays Principle" recommended by the Council of the OECD in 1974, is applied to all sectors of the nuclear industry. Some countries rely upon the accounting standards prevailing in the industry for reporting of nuclear liabilities. Others have established specific government requirements such as the creation of a fund to accumulate provisions for the liabilities, and/or have established companies in charge of radioactive waste disposal and decommissioning of nuclear facilities.

For example, countries such as Belgium, France, Korea and Spain created State agencies or companies responsible for radioactive waste disposal. In Finland, Japan and Sweden, the State provides oversight on and controls the planning, funding and implementation of measures related to radioactive wastes management and disposal.

The very long time during which it is required to ensure that some nuclear waste are isolated from the biosphere has led some governments to take over the responsibility of their final disposal.

Accounting methods

There is a general consensus on the need to recognise future financial liabilities in the accounts of operators in so far as their costs can be reasonably estimated. However, the detailed methods for calculating and reporting liabilities differ from country to country and often from operator to operator in a given country. Two main methods – current value and net present value – and some variation of these are generally used for calculating liabilities. Finland, France, Germany, Japan, Korea and the United States use the current value method while Belgium, Canada, Spain, Sweden and the United Kingdom use the net present value method.

The report provides some details on the accounting and reporting of liabilities as well as on the ways funding for these liabilities are established.

Guaranteeing funds

The organisations which are responsible for the liabilities must have the capacity to pay when the actual expenditures arise. It is especially important to set aside money for covering future liabilities whenever the long-term existence of the organisation generating them is not totally assured or the total assets of the organisation are relatively small as compared to size of the liabilities generated. In any case, general equity considerations and the "Polluter Pays Principle", call for the establishment of measures ensuring that funds are set aside when the future liabilities are generated and are available when the expenditures occur. When an organisation is transferred, e.g. privatisation of utilities, the need arises to identify clearly the nature and extent of pre-existing liabilities, and the organisation responsible for them after the transfer.

The establishment of a fund and guaranteeing of it is generally recognised as a necessary response to the "Polluter Pays Principle". The actual schemes adopted to guarantee the availability of funds when the need arise differ from country to country depending on whether or not the fund is centrally controlled (generally by the State), and whether or not the technical responsibility for the management of the liabilities rest with a central organisation (generally the State).

In some cases, the schemes also vary depending on the source of the liability and the ownership of the company which generates it. The following table summarises the existing schemes for guaranteeing liability funds in the NEA countries that provided information.

Summary of existing schemes for guaranteeing liability funds [1]

Country	Centralised fund, centralised responsibility	Centralised fund, decentralised responsibilities	Guarantees, decentralised responsibilities	Decentralised responsibilities
Australia			√ [2]	
Belgium	√			√ [3]
Canada			√ [2]	√
Finland		√		
France				√
Germany				√
Italy	√			
Japan				√
Korea	√ [4]			√ [3]
Netherlands				√
Spain	√			
Sweden		√		
Switzerland				√
Turkey				√
UK				√
US	√ [4; 5]		√ [3]	

1. In NEA countries which provided information.
2. For mines only.
3. For decommissioning (and spent fuel management in Belgium).
4. For long-lived waste.
5. For enrichment plants.

Concluding remarks and recommendations

The ethical and political need to ensure that the "Polluter Pays Principle" should operate requires that the beneficiaries from electricity and other products or commodities provided by nuclear activities should bear the burden of paying for liabilities arising from these activities.

The study shows that in NEA countries, future financial liabilities arising from nuclear activities are recognised and that schemes are in place for establishing and guaranteeing liability funds. This means that nuclear liabilities are internalised in the cost of nuclear electricity. Since the State has retained jurisdiction over policy issues related to the development, use and control of nuclear energy, it has also taken lead responsibility for promoting schemes ensuring that appropriate arrangements are in place to assure that money will be available when required to pay for radioactive waste disposal and decommissioning of nuclear facilities, in particular if the activities that generated the liabilities would not be producing revenues by the time actual expenses will occur.

Although policies with regard to recognising, reporting and funding liabilities vary from country to country, there are generally supported principles that are reflected in the different country policies and schemes according to the specific national contexts. International studies such as this report should be helpful in illustrating the implementation of general principles in various country-specific conditions.

Since liabilities are not unique to nuclear facilities, some of the principles, concepts and practices described in this report might find application in non-nuclear sectors of the industry.

1. INTRODUCTION

1.1 Background

At the end of 1994, there were some 340 nuclear units connected to the grid within NEA countries [1], representing a total capacity of 283 GWe and generating some 24 per cent of the electricity produced by these countries. Large fuel cycle facilities and uranium mines are operating in several NEA countries. There are also some 40 large nuclear research institutions [2] and several isotope production facilities distributed within NEA countries. The nuclear industry represents a large capital investment, a valuable asset, and contributes significantly to the social, economic and technological development of the countries where it has been established and deployed. It also creates a responsibility to ensure that eventually all facilities are decommissioned and radioactive waste disposed of. The cost and responsibility of returning these sites to something close to their original condition creates what is called a liability. Often the mere existence of the facilities creates a liability. The actual expenditure to discharge that liability may be far in the future. The present report focuses on these "future liabilities". It is a standard practice within the nuclear industry to recognise liabilities and establish measures to ensure that funds will be available when the expenditures will occur.

There is a broad international consensus on standards and codes of practice regarding radioactive waste disposal. All countries engaged in nuclear research, development and industrial activities give particular attention to the safe disposal of radioactive waste, particularly as regards the need to protect humans and the environment now and in the distant future. Broad issues such as ethical aspects of long-lived radioactive waste disposal, public perception of risks and its relation to decision-making have been explored and analysed by NEA [3]. The NEA Radioactive Waste Management Committee published, in 1995, a collective opinion on the environmental and ethical basis of geological disposal of long-lived radioactive waste that presents an international consensus position on these topics [4]. In 1995, the IAEA published, in the Safety Series, a document on safety fundamentals of radioactive waste management that covers basic objectives, concepts and principles to ensure the safe disposal of waste [5]. These documents may serve as a basis for the establishment of appropriate national schemes and mechanisms in different countries that ensure recognition and funding, when needed, of future liabilities arising form nuclear activities.

Both to guarantee that the present beneficiaries of nuclear energy pay for the liabilities and to provide additional confidence that the necessary sums will be available when required, it will generally be appropriate for the responsible organisations to begin making provisions for the sums needed as soon as the liabilities are incurred, which in many cases will be long before the actual expenditure arises. For this reason, it is important that appropriate arrangements should be in place at the time the liabilities are incurred to ensure that the liabilities can be met as the expenditures occur.

The specific arrangements which are appropriate for an organisation may vary depending on its type and ownership and the country's legal and administrative system within which it operates. Factors which might be important include the degree of assurance about the long-term existence of the organisation and the relationship between its total assets and the magnitude of the liability.

In the case where the ownership of the organisation is transferred, a need arises to identify and disclose clearly: the nature and extent of the pre-existing liabilities, the arrangements which are to be made to ensure that funding is available to meet those liabilities, and where the responsibility for them should rest in future. In some cases, the organisation responsible for the liability may be neither a nuclear facility owner nor a radioactive waste producer but an organisation which accepted the responsibility.

Many NEA countries with a nuclear programme have established policies on the treatment of the liabilities. The policies and resultant schemes for preparing against the liabilities vary widely from country to country. Even the practical interpretation of the word "liability" may be different between countries. The measures introduced for establishing financial resources against liabilities arising from nuclear activities might be different, corresponding to, *inter alia*:

- the characteristics (large or small, State-owned or private, obtaining income or not, etc.) of the organisation which is responsible for the liability;
- whether the nuclear activity closed before the establishment of the measures or not;
- the activities for which provisions for liability are necessary.

1.2 Goals and scope of the study

The goal of the study is to provide comprehensive information on the policies and schemes in place in NEA Member countries for recognising, reporting and funding financial liabilities arising from nuclear activities. The scope covers the liabilities in the nuclear industry, including mining, fuel cycle facilities, power generation, research centres and large radioisotope production facilities.

The report covers:

- the main characteristics of liabilities;
- types, sources, value, and timing of occurence[1];
- the types of organisations that generate the liabilities;
- the role of the State both as a regulator and as an operator;
- the methods by which the liabilities are calculated, presented in accounts and updated;
- the means for ensuring that funds are available;
- and finally, a comparative analysis of various approaches, followed by some recommendations.

Most of the information on which this report is based was gathered through a questionnaire circulated to NEA Member countries. The following countries have responded to the questionnaire and/or provided information to the Secretariat: Australia, Belgium, Canada, Finland, France, Germany, Italy, Japan, Korea, the Netherlands, Spain, Sweden, Switzerland, Turkey, the United Kingdom and the United States. It should be pointed out that the responses were received in 1994 and, therefore, refer to data and status as of mid-1994.

---

[1] The scope of the study does **not** include the detailed method of calculating liabilities nor the backgrounds of the calculation.

2. LIABILITIES

2.1 Definition

For the purpose of this report, liabilities are defined as costs which an organisation is expected to have to meet in the future as a consequence of its current or past operations. Liabilities in nuclear activities arise primarily from the costs of spent fuel reprocessing or disposal, radioactive waste management and disposal, and decommissioning of various facilities. For the purpose of this study the term "future" is used as meaning a period of beyond five years. Therefore, liabilities for which systems and procedures are in place to complete within five years or so all the actions needed to satisfy licensing and other regulatory requirements are not considered. Civil liabilities connected with nuclear accidents for which international conventions are in place [6] are not addressed in this report which deals only with liabilities arising from normal operation.

2.2 What are the types of liabilities

There are two main categories of liabilities corresponding to: costs that are generated as installations operate; and those that will arise when installations are taken out of service. The methods used to take account of costs associated to the liabilities vary with the types of liabilities involved.

2.2.1 Liabilities arising from operation

These include reprocessing of spent fuel and management of radioactive waste, including non-reprocessed spent fuel.

The **reprocessing** expenses, which may be considered as part of normal operation, are included in this study because of the substantial amount of time that may elapse before spent fuel is reprocessed and before the resulting products and waste are treated and/or disposed of. In countries that have opted to reprocess at least part of their spent fuel (Belgium, France, Germany, Japan, the Netherlands, Switzerland, the United Kingdom), the full cost of doing so, including that of ultimate disposal of associated waste, is set aside by utilities (or by owners of fissile material) as the fuel is used up in reactors.

The **management of radioactive waste** includes its conditioning, intermediate storage, and final disposal. It is possible to distinguish between low and intermediate-level operating waste from nuclear facilities and high-level waste.

Low and intermediate-level operating waste from nuclear facilities

Where low-level waste disposal facilities are available, it is considered that the cost of conditioning, transporting and storing this type of waste should be treated as operating expenses included in the cost of services rendered, obviating the need to set up provisions for future liabilities.

Where low-level waste disposal facilities are not yet available, it is considered that there is a liability associated with this type of waste, and provisions for the cost of its conditioning, transport, interim storage and eventual disposal are set up in the accounts of those who generate it.

Some short-lived intermediate-level waste may be disposed of along with low-level waste, but for the most part disposal facilities are not available for intermediate-level waste, and provisions for its future disposal are to be set up.

R & D expenditure and capital investment on storage and disposal facilities and the financing thereof are accounted for differently from one country to another. This point will be developed in section 5.3.2.

High-level waste

In countries which have opted for an open fuel cycle, the cost of interim storage, conditioning and direct disposal of spent fuel is set aside as the fuel is used or, in appropriate cases, contributions are made to funds established to cover such costs. Similarly, high-level vitrified waste arising from reprocessing cannot be disposed of in existing facilities, and funds to cover the costs for their interim storage and final disposal have to be set aside. Because of the long lead times before repositories for high-level waste come into use, the overall total cost for interim storage and ultimate disposal of this type of waste is not always known with certainty.

2.2.2   *Liabilities arising from closing down facilities*

These include mine reclamation and decommissioning of nuclear installations, i.e., nuclear fuel cycle facilities, power reactors, research facilities and isotope production plants.

Outlays for major maintenance of facilities, such as the replacement of steam generators, are outside the scope of this study. Such capital maintenance, the cost of which is charged to provisions and spread over a number of years, is common to most industries and therefore not unique to nuclear activities. However, radioactive waste from maintenance activities may generate future liabilities.

The future costs of reclaiming mines, stabilising mill tailings and decommissioning milling plants are provided for by uranium producers and are therefore covered by this study. Such costs are not unique to the nuclear industry, since any mining activity generates similar types of liability.

The future costs of decommissioning nuclear installations include the dismantling of facilities, the decontamination of equipment and the conditioning and disposal of the waste produced by decontamination and dismantling. The installations involved include power plant reactors, research centres and their reactors, fuel cycle plants, isotope production plants, containers and shipping flasks for radioactive products.

For power reactors, the final core of fuel (or a part of it) at the time of closure is treated in a similar way to decommissioning, with the costs for reprocessing or final treatment, storage and disposal being spread over the useful life of the plant.

Although a number of nuclear installations have already been (or are in the process of being), decommissioned, more experience on dismantling and decommissioning large facilities remains to be acquired. However, the costs of the associated liabilities are fairly well estimated [7].

Provisions for this category of liabilities that arise when installations cease to be used are spread over the useful life of the installation or the mine.

2.2.3　Liabilities arising from "historic" activities

Some countries have a third category of future liabilities, which are often referred to as "historic". While they are of the same sort as the first two categories (waste from operation or from the decommissioning of facilities and mines), their distinguishing feature is that they were generated in the past, at a time when inadequate provisions were made for such obligations, which were recognised only later. In this area, and in a sense, each new regulation with retroactive effect "generates" "historic" liabilities.

A regulation may be deemed retroactive if it imposes additional restrictions on past actions that were in compliance with rules existing at the time. For the organisations responsible for the liabilities, this entails constituting further provisions for future "historic" liabilities, which may pose problems with respect to financing and to spreading the burden out over time. A further problem occurs if generators of liabilities have gone out of existence when the historic liabilities are recognised. In that case, it has to be determined who will be responsible for funding the required expenses to cover these liabilities.

2.2.4　Types of liabilities existing in each country

The nature of the future liabilities that each NEA country will have to meet is summarised in Table 2.1, for the countries which provided information.

2.3　Sector of activities

Methods of accounting for future liabilities vary with the sector of activity involved, since the nature of those liabilities can differ from one sector to the next. Moreover, the economic structure and legal status of certain sectors may prompt them to respond differently to the problem of future liabilities of the same type.

For the purpose of this study, the nuclear industry was divided into five sectors: mining and milling, fuel cycle activities, nuclear power plants, research centres and production of radioactive isotopes.

2.3.1　Mining and milling

This sector comprises the mining and milling of uranium and thorium ores. Uranium is widely distributed in nature and is found in concentrations which make it economically feasible to mine. Almost all economically viable ore bodies have grades over 500 parts per million while some significant bodies have concentrations of up to 15 per cent. In some cases, uranium is extracted as a by-product of other metal mining. Uranium ore is mined either by conventional open pit or underground mining methods, and extracted by alkaline or acid leaching processes, or the ore is extracted by in situ leaching.

Future liabilities in this sector arise primarily from the needs for decommissioning of the mine, mill, surface facilities and the waste management areas, such as the waste effluent treatment facilities. The problem has much in common with mine reclamation after other mineral extraction rather than being a particular problem of protection against radioactivity. The radioactive daughter products, such as daughters of ^{230}Th (^{226}Ra and ^{222}Rn) are left with tailings, stabilised and put back into the mine or otherwise disposed of. In all cases, while the volumes of tailings are large, the liabilities associated with their handling and disposal are relatively small and their level of radioactivity is rather low.

Table 2.1 Nature of future liabilities in NEA countries

Country	Reprocessing	Disposal of spent fuel	Disposal of other high-level waste [1]	Disposal of low and intermediate-level waste [2]	Decommis-sioning of facilities [3]	Reclamation of mines
Australia		√ [4]			√	√
Belgium	√	√	√	√	√	
Canada		√		√	√	√
Finland		√			√	
France	√		√	√ [5]	√	√
Germany	√	√		√ [5]	√	√
Italy	√	√		√	√	
Japan	√		√	√ [5]	√	
Korea		√		√	√	√
Netherlands	√	√ [4]	√	√	√	
Spain		√	√ [6]	√ [5]	√	√
Sweden		√			√	
Switzerland	√	√	√	√	√	
Turkey		√ [4]			√	
UK	√		√	√ [7]	√	
US		√		√	√	√

1. Since spent fuel disposal facilities are capable of accepting other high-level waste, this column is filled in only for countries that do not (and will not) have to dispose of spent fuel.
2. This column is filled in for countries in which low and intermediate-level waste disposal facilities are not yet available.
3. Including final closure of waste disposal facilities.
4. For research reactor fuel.
5. Some intermediate waste creates liabilities.
6. From the Vandellos-1 reprocessed spent fuel that will be completed shortly.
7. Most low-level waste is disposed of in existing facilities.

2.3.2   Nuclear fuel cycle

This sector encompasses all processing plants for nuclear fuel, including facilities for converting, enriching, fabricating and reprocessing fuel, as well as for conditioning spent fuel.

Countries such as Canada, France, Japan, the United Kingdom and the United States have facilities to convert uranium into hexafluoride or dioxide for use directly in Gas Cooled Reactors and Pressurised Heavy Water Reactors (CANDUs) or after enrichment in Light Water Reactors and Advanced Gas-Cooled Reactors.

Current enrichment plants are based on the gaseous diffusion process (in France and the United States) or centrifuge process (in Germany, the Netherlands, Japan and the United Kingdom). The production of enriched uranium generates large volumes of depleted uranium (tails). In those countries which do not expect to use these tails for the breeding of further fissile material, the provision of disposal facilities may generate additional liabilities.

Fuel fabrication plants are in operation in many of the NEA Countries. These plants generate liabilities associated mainly with their decommissioning.

At the back-end of the fuel cycle, spent fuel is either disposed of, open cycle, or reprocessed, closed cycle. Where the open cycle has been adopted, liabilities are connected with spent fuel management, storage and disposal; they are under the responsibility of the utility. Where the closed cycle has been adopted liabilities are connected with reprocessing and waste management and disposal. Low, intermediate and high-level wastes arise from the operation and decommissioning of reprocessing plants; high-level waste, mainly separated fission products, are stored at reprocessing plants in a liquid form, vitrified after a number of years and eventually disposed of (vitrified waste is expected to be disposed of in most countries after the year 2020).

2.3.3   Nuclear power plants

Most NEA countries have nuclear power plants that produce electricity. The use of nuclear fuel generates low and intermediate-level waste and spent fuel that can be either reprocessed (closed cycle) or stored in interim storage facilities, at or away from the reactors, prior to disposal as high-level waste (open cycle).

Furthermore, at the end of their operating life, they have to be decommissioned. Three stages of decommmisioning can be considered. Stage 1 implies fuel removal only. Stage 2 demands removal of contaminated and activated components except for the core and heat transport system. Stage 3 means dismantling to "green field" and can take several decades, depending on decommissioning strategies [8]. The precise procedures and time scale of decommissioning the power plant depend on the policy of each country.

Utilities have liabilities connected with spent fuel: either the future cost of ultimate disposal or the cost of reprocessing and storing and disposing of reprocessing waste. The decommissioning of facilities is also a major liability for the sector. In countries that have no disposal facilities, utilities must provide for the future storage of low and intermediate-level waste and eventually for their disposal.

2.3.4   Research centres

Research centres comprise research reactors and various laboratories, and consequently face the same types of liabilities (waste, spent fuel, decommissioning) as the two previous categories. They are set apart in a sector of their own, however, because their legal status and operating procedures are frequently distinct.

2.3.5   Production of radioactive isotopes

This sector comprises production facilities for high level or long-lived radioactive isotopes other than those of uranium or plutonium, such as ^{60}Cobalt, ^{99}Technicium, ^{241}Americium and ^{252}Californium. Their output is generally intended for medicine, research, non-nuclear industries and agriculture. Future liabilities of the producers consist of waste disposal and the dismantling of facilities. The size of producers in this sector tends to be smaller than those in the previous sectors and, therefore, their financial capacity is limited.

If radioisotopes are produced by research centres or fuel cycle companies, the corresponding future liabilities are generally included in the data for those two sectors.

The characteristics of each sector will be analysed in greater detail in chapter 3.

2.4 What is the value of liabilities

Graphs showing the estimated amounts of known future liabilities are included in Annex 1.

For nuclear power plants, the absolute value of liabilities for decommissioning and waste disposal amount to several hundred millions of US dollars for each reactor. Cost estimates for these liabilities are reported in several other studies published by the NEA.

For example, the decommissioning cost estimations for nuclear power plants provided by Member countries for the 1992 study on *Projected Costs of Generating Electricity* [7], range between 15 and 20 per cent of their initial construction costs. The conclusions of this study were that the overall contribution of decommissioning to electricity generation costs was less than 1 per cent (discounted cost) or less than 2 to 3 per cent (undiscounted cost).

Cost estimates for the disposal in geological repositories of high-level waste have been reviewed and analysed in a study published by the NEA in 1993 [9]. Estimates provided by Member countries for encapsulation and disposal of spent fuel or reprocessing waste varied between US$24 000 and US$410 000 per tonne of uranium contained in the spent fuel before reprocessing. These cost estimates, given in 1991 US dollars, are undiscounted. When discounted, at rates and over time periods representative of conditions expected in NEA Member countries, the back-end of the fuel cycle costs were shown to be between about 15 per cent and 30 per cent of the total fuel cycle costs, that is about 3 to 6 per cent of overall electricity generating cost [10].

Some countries have not provided cost estimates for the liabilities arising from their nuclear activities. However, the sensitivity analyses carried out in the NEA studies mentioned above suggest that there is little expectation that the discounted liabilities would differ greatly from the typical estimates that have been given by other NEA Member countries.

In this connection, it is necessary to distinguish between a liability and the provisions set aside for covering the expenses when required. A liability arises as soon as an ultimate need is created to treat or dispose of waste, or to decommission a facility. Provisions are set aside with the intention of providing sufficient money to pay for the treatment and disposal of waste and the decommissioning of facilities by the time these activities will have to be implemented.

Annex 1 shows that there is a variety of patterns with regard to the timing of expenditure on decommissioning and waste disposal. These timings are influenced, principally, by three factors:

- the scenario adopted by each country as to the delay between the closing down of a facility and its final decommissioning, which itself might be affected by policies on recycling/rehabilitating sites;
- the option chosen for waste disposal, i.e., near surface or deep geological repositories;
- the choice of the open or closed fuel cycle. In countries where the closed cycle has been chosen, reprocessing expenses may occur in the relatively near term, while where the open cycle has been adopted, spent fuel disposal expenses will occur later on.

3. ORGANISATIONS INVOLVED

The nuclear activities that generate liabilities pertain to two main lines: activities related to electricity production; and activities related to research and development and radioisotope production. The extraction of uranium also creates liabilities.

The organisations related to electricity production have responsibilities for:

- mining and milling;
- conversion to uranium hexafluoride or dioxide, enrichment and fuel fabrication;
- reactor operation;
- spent fuel management;
- radioactive waste management and disposal;
- decommissioning of facilities.

With respect to the two first items, many countries which have nuclear power plants in operation, do not have any such activities, while the other four items cannot be avoided once nuclear power plants come into operation.

Research and Development is performed to some extent in all NEA countries, most of the time under government sponsorship, while large isotope production facilities exist in only a few NEA countries.

A summary of the activities existing in each country is given in Annex 1.

3.1 Activities related to electricity production

3.1.1 *Mining and milling*

As in any other mining activity, especially open pit mining, liabilities of uranium mining such as decommissioning and conditioning of waste, are part of the integrated rehabilitation process needed to restore the original landscape. The operator of the mine is responsible for the appropriate rehabilitation. In particular cases, such as the German Wismut mine, which was operating in the former Democratic Republic of Germany, the responsibility has been taken over by the government (see section 4.4).

Mine operators in NEA countries range from small specialist mining companies to major international mining conglomerates, as well as subsidiaries of fuel cycle companies. Thus, for example, France and Spain, which have national companies dedicated to fuel cycle activities, in addition to having mines inside their countries, own shares in mines in other countries.

The two main NEA uranium suppliers are Australia and Canada. The case of Australia is very specific; no nuclear industry has been developed and approval for uranium mining has been limited to three sites: the Nabarlek, Olympic Dam and Ranger mines.

Further information on ownership patterns of uranium mines and mills can be found in the "Red Book" [11].

3.1.2   Front-end of the fuel cycle activities

Due to the low radio-toxicity of the natural or slightly enriched uranium, the main liabilities are the disposal of tails from enrichment (unless they are classed as a resource to be used in breeding additional fissile material). In some cases, significant liabilities also arise from the decommissioning of enrichment plants. Other operating liabilities such as radioactive waste generation can be considered as minimal.

Private or State-owned companies have been developed to supply their own national market and, in some cases, joint ventures were created by several countries.

In France and the United Kingdom all the activities are integrated in State-owned companies. Cogema and BNFL or their subsidiaries or related companies, have conversion, enrichment and fuel fabrication plants. Japan has companies which enrich uranium and fabricate fuel. In the United States, the Department of Energy, through a 100 per cent subsidiary (USEC) is the enrichment supplier, while fabrication is done through private companies. Germany, the Netherlands and the United Kingdom have enrichment facilities in a joint-venture (Urenco). Belgium and Spain have shares in Eurodif. Belgium, Canada, Germany, Sweden and Spain have companies that fabricate fuel.

3.1.3   Power generation

The structure of utilities operating nuclear power plants varies between large monopolies operating some 60 reactors (such as EDF in France) to small utilities whose size has entailed their forming consortia to operate a single reactor (in the United States). Therefore, the size of these utilities varies from small companies operating a single reactor and having turnover of the order of US$200 million per annum to companies with diversified sources of generation, operating tens of reactors, with turnover of the order of some US$30 to 40 billion per annum. Many forms of ownership are encountered including full State ownership, shareholder-owned and subsidiaries of broad energy or industrial conglomerates.

3.1.4   Back-end of the fuel cycle activities

In countries where the open cycle has been adopted, the only back-end activity is spent fuel management and disposal which is described in section 3.4 on waste management.

For the closed cycle, organisations are needed for the performance of the reprocessing step and associated activities such as plutonium storage and transport. The activities related to interim storage of spent fuel are dealt with in section 3.4. Within NEA countries, there are two organisations, both of which areState-owned, offering commercial reprocessing services, Cogema in France and BNFL in the United Kingdom. The UKAEA and French CEA also operate smaller reprocessing facilities, mainly for research reactor fuels. Japan intends to operate a commercial reprocessing facility shortly after the year 2000. It will be owned by a consortium of utilities and other industries.

3.2   Research and development

Large nuclear research institutes which have been operated in many NEA countries for several decades, have generally been established by States and, therefore, States are responsible for the liabilities arising from their operation. However, some nuclear research centres and institutes have diversified over time and parts of them have been sold to the private sector. In these cases, it has generally been arranged that the liabilities arising from past activities should remain with the State. Further information on nuclear research centres in NEA countries might be found in the NEA publication on *Past trends and current state of Nuclear Institutes* [2].

Several research centres within the European Union were taken under the auspices of the European Commission even though they were originally established as national institutions. Other research establishments (e. g. Institute for Transuranium Elements in Karlsruhe, Germany) were set up as European institutions. There is a variety of agreements which set out, among others, the responsibilities for waste management and disposal and decommissioning of the facilities.

3.3 Radioisotope production

In parallel with research on nuclear power production, research was also undertaken on other industrial and medical uses of radiation. This has led to the establishment of a number of organisations specialising in the production of radionuclide sources for use in diagnostic and therapeutic medical applications and a wide range of industrial applications such as process control, non-destructive quality control, industrial radiography and food irradiation. Liabilities in this sector derive from waste arising from the manufacture of such sources, the management and disposal of spent sources and the decommissioning of the facilities in which they are produced. The radionuclide production facilities have generally remained in the government sector while the packaging, marketing and other activities have been privatised, thus the future liabilities rest with the governments. The position with regard to the disposition of radioactive sources that have entered the market varies between countries. The following notes illustrate briefly some of the features of the isotope production sector, by way of examples from Canada and Sweden.

In Canada, there is one private sector company which is the prime supplier of radioisotope products and technology. It also serves customers around the world in radiation processing and radio-pharmaceuticals. The company has two radioisotope processing facilities, and a research and demonstration irradiation facility. At present, there are about 4 000 radioisotope licences in Canada for the users in hospitals, universities and industries. Operating waste from these users, including spent sealed sources, are shipped to and stored at the Chalk River Laboratories of Atomic Energy of Canada Limited.

In Sweden, sealed radiation sources are not produced commercially, but are still widely used for technical, medical, scientific and educational purposes. There are also smoke alarms containing modest ^{241}Am sources in most Swedish homes. Spent sealed radiation sources with activities worthy of consideration are usually sent for destruction and storage to the Studsvik RadWaste AB, a privatised branch of the former State-owned nuclear research establishment, either directly from a user or via the provider. The sources will eventually end up in the Swedish final repository for low and intermediate-level waste, SFR at Forsmark. Solitary discarded domestic smoke alarms may still be mixed with the ordinary household trash. Larger numbers discarded at the same time, as well as smoke detector systems containing several sources should, however, be regarded as radioactive waste and thus handled in the way mentioned above.

3.4 Waste management

Radioactive waste are produced in all radioactive related activities, even though the major part of the activity contained in these waste come from the operation of the nuclear power plants and from the direct disposal or reprocessing of the spent fuel.

Waste management objectives are to secure an acceptable level of protection for human health and the environment, taking into account possible effects beyond national borders and the protection of future generations. These objectives are met by the immobilisation of activity and its isolation from the human environment for a period of time and in such conditions that any liberation of radionuclides contained in the waste will not create an unacceptable radiological risk to people and the environment.

In order to attain these objectives, it is necessary to use a combination of engineered and natural barriers between the waste and the environment in such a way that radionuclides are retained or that their release is retarded until their activity has decayed to acceptable levels.

Table 3.1 gives a classification of radioactive waste, according to their type, characteristics, origin and form of disposal [12]. The classification reflects the activity and the half-life of the radionuclides contained in the waste and the fact that they may be disposed of in deep geological formations or surface facilities. In practice, for regulatory purposes, national waste classification may, and often does differ, from the one given in Table 3.1.

In many NEA countries, there is a central organisation which has responsibility for some or all waste management functions. Such organisations exist in Belgium, France, Germany, Korea, the Netherlands, Spain, Sweden, Switzerland, the United Kingdom and the United States, and will exist in Finland from the beginning of 1996.

This does not mean that all those organisations have the same level of responsibilities. Some organisations have responsibility for limited categories of waste. For example, Nirex in the United Kingdom is responsible for the disposal of intermediate and some low-level waste, but not for high-level waste. Regional compacts in the United States are responsible only for low-level waste. Others, such as ENRESA in Spain, have responsibilities covering the management of all the waste including the decommissioning of nuclear facilities.

The responsibilities of such an organisation could include:

a) handling and conditioning of radioactive waste;

b) siting, design, construction, operation and closing of interim and final disposal facilities for high, low and intermediate-level waste;

c) management of the activities derived from the decommissioning of nuclear and radioactive installations;

d) setting-up of systems for collection, transfer and transportation of radioactive waste;

e) conditioning, when required, of the tailings arising from uranium mining and milling, in a safe and definitive manner;

f) ensuring the long-term management of any waste disposal facility;

g) carrying out the necessary technical, economical and financial studies taking into account the deferred cost of radioactive waste management.

The ownership of organisations responsible for waste management varies from country to country. In some countries such as Belgium, France and Spain, the State owns such organisations, while in other countries such as Germany, Japan and the United Kingdom, they are owned by a consortium of waste producers, which may itself entail part ownership by the State.

Table 3.1 Radioactive waste classification

Category	Characteristics	Origin [1]	Disposal options
Low level	– Low β/γ activity – Insignificant α activity – Insignificant heat production	– Liquid waste and their solidification products – Solid waste from power plants – α-emitting waste from fuel manufacturing – Decommissioning waste	Near surface repositories
Intermediate level	– Significant β/γ activity – Low α activity – Low heat production	– Solidified liquid waste from reprocessing – Waste from power plants contaminated with tritium – Decommissioning waste from power plants	– Shallow land repositories [2] – Deep geological repositories
Alpha bearing	– Low β/γ activity – Significant α activity – Low heat production	– Intermediate liquid waste from reprocessing – Fuel element cladding and metallic parts/closed cycle – Decommissioning waste	Deep geological repositories
High level	– High β/γ activity – Significant α activity – High heat production	– High-level liquid waste from reprocessing – Solidified material from reprocessing – Spent fuel/ open cycle	Deep geological repositories

1. The list of origins for each category is illustrative and not exhaustive.
2. Disposal with or without engineered barriers, above or below the ground surface where the final protective covering is of the order of a few metres thick.

4. THE ROLE OF THE STATE

4.1   Main legislative actions

The State has to ensure that the consequences of its energy policy will not harm present and future generations. In the case of present generations, it is the responsibility of the State to establish and enforce regulations related to the use of radioactive materials and radiation protection. With respect to future generations, the State has to assure that actions are undertaken to ensure that the environment is not unduly affected. But more than those technical and managerial actions, it is also necessary that economic liabilities foreseen in the future decades be guaranteed with money provided during operation of nuclear facilities.

In 1974, the Council of OECD recommended the application by governments of the fundamental "Polluter Pays Principle" defined in the early 1970s. This principle is generally applied for allocating costs of pollution prevention and control measures introduced by the public authorities. It means that the cost of these measures should be reflected in the costs and prices of goods or services which cause pollution in production and/or consumption. This principle is applied to all sectors of the nuclear industry.

In order to fulfil their commitments in this regard, States have generally acted to:

- ensure that due account is taken of future liabilities at the time when the activities giving rise to them are undertaken; or

- establish, as a State responsibility, the control and/or operation of some or all those activities; or

- take responsibility for the management and disposal of "historic" waste.

With respect to the first item, many countries have regulations on the funding of the liabilities incurred, while for the second, many countries have determined that the State, itself or through some type of participation in a company, should be involved in the design and operation of disposal activities. For the third item, States are the last resort to bear the costs of management and disposal of "historic" waste whenever applicable.

4.2   Securing financial arrangements

As was indicated in section 4.1, it is important that appropriate arrangements be in place at the time the liabilities are incurred to ensure that they can be met when they mature.

While there are countries where no specific government requirements exist, other than accepted accounting standards, some have rules established by the government for creating funds to pay the liabilities and for creating companies to undertake waste disposal and decommissioning work.

In countries where the State owns industrial groups operating a large number of power plants or fuel cycle facilities, it has not generally been considered necessary to impose a requirement for such funds. For example, this is the case of France where EDF is the sole operator of nuclear power plants and Cogema the fuel cycle company. In the United Kingdom, Nuclear Electric, Scottish Nuclear, and BNFL fulfil similar roles.

In the case of Japan, even though the State does not act as owner, the nuclear share of the utilities, added to their size, has given enough guarantee for the government to be able to rely primarily on accounting standards. Legislation has established rules controlling the funds reserved for decommissioning of power plants and reprocessing spent fuel.

Other countries such as Belgium, Finland, Korea, Spain, Sweden and the United States have created, by law, funding systems so as to assure that outside the regular balance sheet of the operators, i.e. not directly accessible to them, funds are available for the safe handling and final disposal of some or all of the waste arising and in some cases the decommissioning of the nuclear facilities. In Korea and Belgium the fund is envisaged only for the disposal of the waste and does not include the dismantling of the nuclear facilities which remains under the financial responsibility of the utility; in these two cases, this fund is managed by a State-owned organisation.

In Belgium, the State and the utilities reached an agreement in 1985 by which the utilities constitute the necessary provisions to cover dismantling and decommissioning costs. The provisions are under the supervision of the "Control Committee for Gas and Electricity". The annual appropriations are revised every five years.

In Canada, the utilities operating nuclear power plants are owned by the provincial governments, and note in their financial statements the estimated costs for decommissioning and disposal of radioactive waste. The Atomic Energy Control Board, the competent authority, has issued a Regulatory Policy Document by which licensees must identify costs for decommissioning as early as the planning and design stage of a nuclear facility. A new regulation is expected to be introduced soon to replace the existing Atomic Energy Control Act. The new Act and the supporting regulations will include the need for the generator of liabilities to provide financial assurance for decommissioning to the satisfaction of prevailing regulations. For the case of uranium and thorium mining, a revised regulation was promulgated in 1994 in order to ensure that sufficient funds will be available for decommissioning.

In Finland and Sweden, the holder of a power plant license is responsible for ensuring that all measures are adopted for the safe handling and final disposal of nuclear waste, (or nuclear material which is not to be reused) generated by the activities, and for the safe decommissioning of facilities. This has led in Sweden, to the Financing Act of 1981, and in Finland to the Nuclear Energy Act of 1988. These laws are intended to guarantee that funds are available when different measures in the nuclear waste management programme are carried out. To achieve this, the reactor owners pay to the State a fee related to the energy supplied from each reactor. The fund is administered by the central government authority: in Finland through the Ministry of Trade and Industry with the State Nuclear Waste Management Fund (VYR); in Sweden, through the Swedish Nuclear Power Inspectorate, SKI. VYR refunds assets in its fund which exceed the defined liabilities. The liabilities cover all waste types and all waste management measures including R & D. Guided by the Financing Act, SKI decides on reimbursement to the nuclear power utilities of costs relating to management of spent nuclear fuel, the decommissioning of nuclear plants, and for R & D on these activities.

In Germany, the "Endlagervorausleistungverordnung" (Repository Advance Payment Ordinance) of 1982 establishes a funding mechanism which entitles the Bundesamt für Strahlenschutz (BfS, Federal Bureau for Radiation Protection) to collect advance payments from the waste producers to cover future costs for repository R & D, land purchase and legal actions, repository planning, construction and operation. Concerning decommissioning costs, the "German Commercial Law" requires that money is set aside annually during the operating life-time of the facility. Responsibility for the fund is retained by the owner of the facility who has to follow accepted accounting standards in preparing annual accounts. The operator/owner of the facility has to justify the provisions to supervision boards, e.g. supervisory auditors, certified public accountants.

In Spain, the law considers that the cost for disposal of the waste arising from nuclear power plants and their decommissioning is an external cost, and thus not the liability of the licence holder. Those responsibilities for radioactive waste disposal and decommissioning of nuclear power plants rest with a State-owned company. To ensure funding of that company, the government approves a General Radioactive Waste Plan which include both technical actions to be taken and the financial requirements during the expected life of the power plants. These external costs, revised annually, are reflected in the electricity prices paid by the consumers.

In the United States there are funding mechanisms for the management of spent fuel and decommissioning of the power plants. In the case of spent fuel the operator has to pay the Department of Energy (DOE) a levy on each kWh produced, while a financial assurance must guarantee the decommissioning of the radioactive portion of a nuclear power plant.

4.3   Operating activities

Often the discussion on waste turns more on the ethics and sociology than on the technical aspects. The fact that some radioactive waste may last for many thousands of years has persuaded some governments that radioactive waste management cannot be left in the hands of the private sector. So laws have been created, putting responsibility for waste management in the State's hands.

Belgium, France, Korea and Spain have created by law, State agencies or companies responsible for disposal sites. In the case of Spain, that company has among its duties not only the management of the waste but also the decommissioning of the nuclear installations, while in the other three countries, this is the responsibility of the operator.

In Canada, the governments of the provinces are the owners of the utilities owning the nuclear power plants. Mining and milling and fuel cycle facilities are privately owned. The operators are responsible for decommissioning and waste management and disposal. The State has not assumed any waste management responsibility except for "historic" waste (see section 4.4).

In Finland, Japan, the Netherlands, Sweden and the United Kingdom, as in Canada, the State does not act as operator. Nevertheless, in Finland, Japan and Sweden the State plays an important role as it oversees and controls the planning and implementation of measures relating to nuclear waste management, and ensures that they are carried out in a timely and proper matter. This requires a close degree of co-operation between the organisation for the handling and disposal of radioactive waste, the State and the nuclear power utilities. If the waste producer does not fulfil his responsibilities to plan and implement the waste management measures properly, the State has a right, according to Finnish and Swedish law, to carry out those measures by using the assets of the fund.

In the Netherlands, the State has a minor share in the COVRA, a joint venture between the major radioactive waste producers and the government. Its statutory task is to execute the radioactive waste policy of the Dutch Government which will take over the control of the waste as well as the responsibility for their disposal in the case of bankruptcy or termination of COVRA.

In the United Kingdom, even though the State as such does not intervene, State-owned companies related to nuclear activities have established a private company, Nirex, in order to develop and operate disposal facilities for medium-level and some low-level waste.

In Germany, the operators of nuclear power plants, in order to retain their license, have to give evidence each year, six years in advance, that spent fuel management is guaranteed, e.g. through reprocessing contracts. The *Atomgesetz* (Atomic Law) which regulates construction and operation of nuclear facilities is implemented by the Federal States (Bundeslander) by awarding licenses while the Federal Republic oversees and controls execution of the Atomgesetz. The BfS on behalf of the Bundesministerium für Umwelt, Naturschutz und Reaktorsicherheit (BMU, Federal Ministry of Environment Protection and Reactor Safety) pursues construction of radioactive waste repositories and has commissioned the Deutsche Gesellschaft zum Bau und Betrieb von Endlagern für Abfallstoffe mbH (DBE) to construct and eventually operate these repositories. The nuclear industry has established the Gesellschaft für Nuklear-Service (GNS), a company that takes care of all waste and spent fuel management obligations.

In the United States, the Low-level Radioactive Policy Act of 1980 placed the responsibility for low-level radioactive waste on the States, while the Federal Government is responsible for high-level waste pursuant to the Nuclear Waste Policy Act of 1982. In some cases, several States have created "regional compacts" responsible for low-level waste management at the regional level.

Table 4.1 summarises the situation with regard to the operating bodies for waste management and decommissioning in those NEA countries which have a nuclear power programme and provided information.

4.4   Historic waste

Some countries have to consider the management of waste produced before legislation was sufficiently settled or arising from new regulations on nuclear electricity generation and/or fuel cycle activities. In such cases, the State had to take as its own responsibility the management and associated costs for the so called "historic waste".

There can also exist some situations where wastes were produced, but the producer organisation has ceased its activities and does not exist any more. In such cases, the "responsible producer" will not be able to finance the liabilities he has incurred and the State has to intervene and be responsible for both management and financing.

In Belgium, when the old Eurochemic complex, a multinational research project, was closed the State had to cover the cost of waste management, decommissioning and site restoration. These activities have been carried out by the State agency established for waste management.

In Canada, a large proportion of the existing inventory of low-level waste consists of historic waste. These were managed in a manner no longer considered acceptable and for which the original producer could not be held responsible. The Federal Government has assumed the responsibility for the management of these historic wastes. In 1982, the government established the Low-Level Radioactive Waste Management Office as the Federal agent responsible for the clean up of sites contaminated by these wastes. Approximately 90 per cent of Canada's current inventory of historic waste are in one localised area of the province of Ontario. These wastes, which largely resulted from the radium industry and the early days of the uranium industry and contain uranium, radium, arsenic, and thorium as well as other associated heavy metals, were generated at a time when waste management practices were not comparable to those required to meet modern standards.

In Germany, after the reunification in 1990, the nuclear industry facilities of the former Democratic Republic of Germany came under the jurisdiction of the Federal Republic of Germany. These facilities included the nuclear power plants of Greifswald and Rheinsberg, the uranium mine of

Wismut and the waste repository of Morsleben. While the uranium mine and the power plants are undergoing decommissioning with funds supplied by the Federal Government, first steps have been taken to obtain an operation licence for the low and intermediate-level waste repository of Morsleben beyond the year 2000.

Table 4.1 Waste management and decommissioning of nuclear power facilities [1]

Countries with funds under government control	Operating body	
	Waste management	Decommissioning
Belgium [2]	State agency	− −
Finland	Operator under State supervision	Operator under State supervision
Korea	State agency	Operator
Spain	State owned company	State owned company
Sweden	Operator under State supervision	Operator under State supervision
Switzerland	Private comp. (State participation)	Operator
US (spent fuel only)	Federal agency	

Countries with no regulated funds	Operating body	
	Waste management	Decommissioning
Belgium [2]	− −	Operator
Canada [3]	Operator (Prov. Gov. owned)	Operator
France2	State agency	Operator
Germany	Operator	Operator
Italy [4]	Former operator	Former operator
Japan [5]	Operator	Operator
Netherlands	Private comp. (State participation)	Operator
UK [6]	Operator	Operator
US (all but spent fuel)	State government (only disposal)	

1. Within NEA countries having a nuclear power programme and which provided information.

2. Funds under government control for waste management; no regulated funds for decommissioning and spent fuel management.

3. The responsibility for implementing disposal of nuclear fuel waste has not been assigned yet.

4. After the shut down of all nuclear power plants, the national utility (ENEL) has been assigned by the State the responsibility for liabilities.

5. Although the future expenditure on decommissioning of nuclear power plants is accounted as a liability (i.e. a reserve) in the balance sheets of the electricity utilities, these companies are required to obtain government approval for the annual re-evaluation of the expected cost. With regard to HLW disposal and related matters decisions on procedures and the entity to be in charge have not been taken yet.

6. Although the operator is responsible for waste management and decommissioning operations, the State provides funding for that work where the liabilities arise from work undertaken in pursuit of government nuclear programmes.

In Italy, the nuclear power plants were closed down in 1987 following a referendum. Funds for liabilities had been set aside by the owner of those plants during their operation. However, the accumulated fund was not sufficient to cover fully the future expenses as they were estimated at the time of shut down. The State and the national utility ENEL have been responsible for raising the necessary additional fund and ensuring that decommissioning and waste disposal activities are carried out in due course.

In Sweden, a special act was passed in 1988 regarding the financing of the management of certain types of radioactive waste from the old research site in Studsvik. Under this act, the reactor licencees are responsible for paying a special fee to the State for managing the waste from older test installations and for the decommissioning of these installations. This act applies in particular to installations which were once constructed in connection with the introduction of nuclear power into Sweden and to the cost of restoring the former Ranstad uranium mining site.

In the United Kingdom, the UKAEA, and some parts of BNFL, undertook research and other nuclear work as a part of the government nuclear programmes. Whilst the government provides the funds required to meet the associated decommissioning and waste management liabilities, under the terms of the relevant nuclear site licences, the operator remains responsible for carrying out the work and for ensuring the safe operation of the sites. Where the government has accepted financial responsibility for the liabilities, the operator is not required to make provision in its accounts for that work. In addition when the majority of the UK electricity industry was privatised in 1989, the relevant legislation (the Electricity Act) included provision for grants to be paid by the government, where necessary and subject to limitations as to the total available, in respect of qualifying expenditure on decommissioning and waste management liabilities.

In the United States, the government has taken the financial responsibility for the management of "commingled" tailings resulting from mining and milling activities carried out for the dual purpose of producing uranium for the commercial market and for the government nuclear programme. Title X of the "Energy Policy Act" of 1992 authorised DOE to provide Federal financial assistance to the owners of active milling sites for management and remediation of mill tailings that were generated under contracts with the US Government. Remedial costs reimbursable under Title X of the "Energy Policy Act" include, among other things, decontamination, decommissioning and reclamation costs, provided that claims are supported by reasonable documentation. Each mill owner is individually responsible, but not obligated, to submit a reimbursement claim. Subsequent claims can be made annually up to the end of 2002.

5. RECOGNITION OF LIABILITIES

5.1 Methods of recognition

Apart from the basic principles accepted in all NEA countries, detailed methods for calculating future liabilities vary from one country to the next and often between operators in the same country. This study is concerned with how a liability is recognised once its future cost has been estimated, not with the detail of the calculation of that cost. Nevertheless, the principles of the two main methods of calculation used are briefly presented and compared below for background information.

Current value

This method consists of evaluating a future liability in terms of what it would cost to meet it today. That figure is then adjusted annually for inflation and periodically revised to take account of technological or regulatory changes affecting costs. In this method, the value ascribed to a future liability is independent of the time at which the expense will actually be incurred. It is used by Finland, Germany, France, Japan (for decommissioning), Korea and the United States.

Net present value

This method consists of estimating the current cost of a liability and then projecting it into the expected time frame. An estimation is then made of the net present value of the relevant cash flows on the basis of an assumed discount rate. Like the previous method, this one also involves periodic revisions to account for inflation and technological change.

In this method, the actual timing of liabilities is crucial, since, for a given estimate, the later a liability is assumed to be incurred, the more it will be discounted and thus the lower its net present value (NPV). The net present value of a liability recognised in this manner is lower than if it were calculated using the current value method, but provides a more realistic representation of the funding demands upon the operator over time. The NPV method is used by Australia (for the Ranger mine), Belgium, Canada, Japan (in the case of reprocessing of spent fuel), Spain, Sweden and the United Kingdom.

Spain, Sweden and the United Kingdom make their calculations in **constant** money values and apply fixed discount rates corresponding to **real** returns, net of tax, on long-term financial investments (Spain, 3.5 per cent; Sweden, 2.5 per cent; the United Kingdom, 2 per cent). Varying degrees of conservatism are built into the discount rate assumptions to ensure that the estimates are properly prudent in accounting terms. In Belgium, the State-owned company ONDRAF/NIRAS is using a discount rate close to the return on risk less assets of 2 per cent per annum in real terms, while private companies are using their own internal rates of return.

It should be noted that, in the United Kingdom, producers of radioisotopes use the current value method.

In the case of Canadian utilities, calculations are made in **current** dollars. Present costs are first increased in line with projected inflation, then deflated to their net present value using a discount rate corresponding to a **nominal** rate of return on financial investments, which is different for each enterprise. Some mining companies use the current value method, probably to be consistent with the accounting practices of their foreign parents.

The Netherlands is an interesting case in point, since the utility NVGKN uses the current value method, while the industrial group Urenco, the research centre ECN and the body responsible for waste management use net present value with different discount rates.

Comparison of the two methods

The choice of method by individual companies is largely conditioned by the prevailing legal requirements and accounting practices in their own country. The following differences between the two methods are noteworthy.

The **current value method**, results in the provisions accumulating more rapidly than the net present value method. With the current value method:

- for future operating costs, the entire amount of a future liability is provided for as soon as it appears and assumptions as to when it will be incurred are immaterial;

- for liabilities that are spread out over time, such as decommissioning, provisions are set up through equal (except for inflation) annuities, allowing to calculate, and reflect in prices, the full cost of electricity generation. Annuities are independent of the assumed lead time between shut down and decommissioning of the facility;

- provisions are set up faster, which is advantageous in countries where such provisions are tax-deductible;

- the interest generated by the accumulated provisions represent an additional taxable revenue.

Although the current value method gives greater certainty that required sums can be provided when required, it may be over-prudent through lack of recognition of the economic value of the provisions made over time.

The **net present value method** determines the amount to be set aside each year in order to cover the future liability when incurred. It views provisions from a "savings" perspective and offers the advantage of tailoring accounting provisions to the financing to be accumulated by a given date. This method:

- is more sensitive to assumptions regarding the precise timing of future liabilities, as well as to projected real returns on the capital set aside;

- accumulates funds more slowly than the current value method.

5.2 Presentation

Methods for presenting future liabilities reflect the diversity of policy with respect to the corresponding responsibilities.

In countries where responsibility is retained by operators, they are required to set up balance sheet provisions to cover these future liabilities. They must justify the amounts of such provisions to their supervisory bodies (boards of directors), independent auditors or supervisory authorities. As a result, estimations of total costs are checked when accounts of the entities responsible are audited. This system is the most widespread, since it is found in Canada, France, Japan (concerning the costs of decommissioning power plants and reprocessing spent fuel), Germany, the Netherlands and the United Kingdom, and in Belgium for spent fuel management and decommissioning. In the United Kingdom, the major operators each identify the total undiscounted costs in notes to the accounts as well as the discounted balance sheet provisions.

At the other end of the spectrum, some countries have transferred responsibility for end-of-cycle operations to specialised agencies, which are financed by fees paid by the generators of waste. Here, estimates of future costs are regularly submitted to (normally State-run) supervisory bodies, which either set or propose the amount of fees that generators will have to pay. Since these payments effectively transfer responsibility for future financial liabilities, those liabilities no longer appear on the generators' financial statements. This system exists in Spain (except for mines) and in the United States for spent fuel disposal.

Between these two extremes lies a whole range of intermediate systems.

In Sweden, utilities carry future liabilities for the operating waste (low-level and intermediate waste) on their balance sheet, because they have the direct economical responsibility for these forms of waste. For future costs controlled under the Financing Act (for spent fuel and decommissioning) and for which the utilities have made payments to the State, the utilities identify the accumulated funded fees in an off-balance sheet appendix, showing payments to date, interest earned, and reimbursements received to cover expenses.

In Korea, the KEPCO utility sets up balance sheet provisions for future liabilities. Fees paid to the body responsible for managing nuclear waste are subsequently charged to these provisions.

In Finland, utilities pay fees, which affect their earnings, to a guarantee fund. In addition, they must disclose, as an off-balance sheet commitment, the portion of future costs not covered by the amounts available in the fund. Securities or guarantees intended to cover these amounts are also indicated in balance sheet appendices of the utilities or their owners.

A special case of a different sort is that of countries in which research centres are run by governmental agencies. These bodies generally receive annual appropriations from the national budget and are therefore bound to the public accounting rules of their respective States. However, it is not always possible for them to post provisions for future liabilities. To the extent that governments are responsible for funding the future liabilities generated by these bodies, the amounts needed to cover them will be released at the appropriate time as part of the annual appropriation. For information purposes, the overall amount of a government's future liabilities may be listed as an off-balance sheet commitment (France and the United Kingdom), details of which are submitted separately to the ministry in charge (the United Kingdom).

5.3   Accounting for the accumulation of funds

Having examined the methods by which future liabilities are recognised and presented, we should now turn to how provisions for these liabilities are set up.

We have just seen that the nuclear industry may, depending on the country, retain responsibility for the future liabilities it generates, or it may transfer that responsibility to specialised bodies by paying them fees.

We shall now examine, in turn, the way the industry constitutes provisions and how it accounts for the money paid out to bodies specialised in end-of-cycle operations.

5.3.1 Constitution of accounting provisions

5.3.1.1 Appropriation to provisions

In most countries the nuclear industry (utilities, mining companies, fuel cycle industries) remains liable for end of cycle costs. Therefore, under accountancy rules, the responsible companies have to set up accounting provisions to meet these liabilities.

The rules vary depending on the nature of the liabilities:

For spent fuel reprocessing, provisions are based on the full cost of reprocessing. The provisions are accumulated as and when the fuel is used up in reactors and they are disbursed when the spent fuel is actually reprocessed (Belgium, France, Germany, Japan, the Netherlands, the United Kingdom). An exception is the final core at the time of plant closure where the costs of reprocessing are generally spread over the reactor lifetime.

For low-level radioactive waste, accounting procedures vary from one country to the next. Some countries take the view that these costs form part of routine operating costs, and provided the waste is dispatched for disposal only a few months after the date of waste production, there is no need to make any special provisions (France, Japan, Sweden, the United Kingdom).

Other countries set aside provisions for disposal of low-level waste, mostly providing for total liabilities at the time of waste production.

In the case of **intermediate- and high-level radioactive waste**, interim storage is generally lengthy until final disposal sites become available. Consequently, provisions are almost always made for this type of waste. As a rule they are made for the total estimated cost at the time of waste production. The largest provisions concern spent fuel for countries which have not opted for reprocessing.

In Germany, no distinction is made between provisions for high-level or low-level waste. Both are accumulated over the useful life of a fuel assembly in a power plant, some three years.

For plant decommissioning, the provisions are generally calculated by spreading out future liabilities over the estimated service life of the facilities or some defined shorter period. This ensures that by the end of the facility life, a provision equal to the cost of dismantling would be available. The amount of the provision must be equal to the net present value or to the current value of the total cost depending on the methods used (see section 5.1).

The amount to be obtained is usually spread over the plant's service life using one of the two approaches described below for the current value method.

One approach is to calculate the appropriation to be made in a given year by dividing the total cost of decommissioning (as estimated in the year considered) minus the existing provisions by the number of years remaining before the end of the lifetime of the facility.

Another approach used is to calculate the appropriation of a given year by dividing the total cost of decommissioning (as estimated in the year considered) by the lifetime of the facility, multiply this number by the number of years from the beginning of the appropriation and subtract from the result the existing provisions.

The two approaches would be equivalent if the total estimated cost of decommissioning were to remain constant over time. However, in practice, this cost varies through inflation and occasionally due to revised estimates following technical or regulatory changes. The effect of the first approach is to spread out the impact of cost revisions over the remaining lifetime of the facility. On the other hand, the second formula assigns to the year of the revision the catch-up effect of this revision on the whole provisions already made.

The first approach seems more appropriate when cost revisions are made owing to technical or regulatory changes. In that case, it seems fair to spread out the additional provisions over the remaining lifetime of the facility and not to assign the catch-up effect on the provisions already made to the year of the revision.

The second approach appears to be more appropriate for taking inflation into account. It seems more logical to take into account the total impact of inflation each given year rather than to spread it out over the remaining lifetime of the facility.

In practice, only one of these approaches is used in a given country (or for a given facility) whatever the cause of the cost revision, i.e. technical or regulatory change or inflation.

At the end of the period over which the financing is spread out, i.e. usually after plant shutdown, the provision is equal to the total decommissioning cost, in current or net present value. Further additions (or deductions) will have to be made to take into account inflation or changes in estimates occurring between shut-down and actual decommissioning. Where provisions are in net present value, an appropriation will also have to be made each year for adding annual interest.

Provisions for mine reclamation follow the same rules as those for plant decommissioning. More specifically, some countries spread out the provisions on a straight-line basis (France) while others do so in proportion to the mining output (Canada).

The appropriations to the above described provisions of course merely concern the bodies retaining final liability for these costs and not those having transferred the liability to third parties through the payment of fees. Nor does this concern government agencies which cannot set up these provisions owing to their status of public establishment funded through the State budget.

5.3.1.2 Counterpart on the assets

The balance sheet entry of a provision for future liabilities amounts to recognition of a corresponding debt. The provision is increased through an appropriation considered as a cost for the financial year to be deducted from profits.

The deduction diminishes distribution possibilities, which is tantamount to setting up a cash reserve for these future liabilities. As a rule, such funds are reinvested in the current account of the firms concerned (Belgium, Canada, France, Korea, the Netherlands, the United Kingdom). These sums are therefore spread among the various components on the assets side without any special treatment.

5.3.1.3 Disbursement of provisions

As a general rule the provisions made are disbursed when the liabilities materialise as the corresponding work is done, or in some cases when relevant contractual payments fall due. In Belgium and Korea the disbursement of provisions corresponds to payments to the body responsible for end of cycle operations.

5.3.1.4 Taxation

The taxation arrangements for these provisions in each country concerned, cannot be reviewed in detail within the scope of this study. Nevertheless the general issue of tax deductibility of the provisions is worth examining.

The deductibility or non-deductibility of the provisions is likely to be a factor which affects the organisations' choice of the method to be used for building up the provisions. Tax deductibility is an incentive to speed up the rate at which the provisions are made.

5.3.2 Financing bodies responsible for waste management and decommissioning

Once the future liabilities have been recognised in the accounts of the bodies which generate these liabilities, mechanisms have to be put in place to finance the organisations responsible for implementing waste management. The financing of bodies responsible for waste management and decommissioning vary from country to country as illustrated by the examples given below.

In Spain, ENRESA evaluates all estimated costs, year by year, for all existing installations as well as future projects. The evaluation takes into account:

- the service life of nuclear power plants;
- the schedule of operations (disposal of low-level waste, transport of spent fuel for interim storage, conditioning and disposal of spent fuel);
- R & D;
- investments for the necessary installations and all ancillary projects;
- decommissioning of power plants five years following the end of life;
- operational costs for the disposal of low-level waste, conditioning, transport and disposal of spent fuel;
- closing down the disposal facility and security arrangements;
- compensation to neighbouring communities.

The fund set up by ENRESA through a levy on electricity sales is reinvested in national stock or bonds of large firms so that it can be recovered in due course.

The main advantage of this system is that liabilities of nuclear power plants are covered directly by electricity consumers and that funds are available whenever necessary, independently from the electricity producers. Not even a bankruptcy of an electricity producer could seriously affect the system. By means of an annual budgetary review, the firm responsible for expenditure ensures that any calculation error could be put right in time.

Spain represents one end of a spectrum of different arrangements. At the opposite end are arrangements such as those in France, Germany and the United Kingdom, whereby provisions accumulated by the "generator" of the liabilities are released to pay for appropriate services as and when those services are provided. While this produces a good match between income and expenditure streams for decommissioning operations, reprocessing of spent fuel and intermediate stages of waste management (e.g. conditioning and packaging of waste), it leaves a substantial miss-match in cases where a heavy investment is required to develop waste disposal facilities (e.g. deep geological repositories). Additional arrangements may be implemented to overcome this mis-match. In the United Kingdom, for example, the organisation responsible for providing deep geological disposal facilities is owned by the major waste producers and is financed by them, together with contributions from some lesser producers of waste.

Other funding methods are also possible. In Finland and Sweden, a separate fund is built up from charges on waste generators, the fund being used to defray all the subsequent expenses by the waste management organisation. In the United States, a levy on nuclear electricity sales provides a fund held by the organisation responsible for high-level waste management and disposal (USDOE).

6. MEANS OF GUARANTEEING FUNDS

The need to guarantee funds for financing future liabilities arises from the agreed "Polluter Pays Principle" which states that the present beneficiaries of nuclear activities, e.g. nuclear generated electricity, should bear the responsibility and costs of the liabilities created by these activities, e.g. waste disposal (see chapter 4). In order to meet this principle, mechanisms must be set up to ensure that funds are available when payment is required to cover the cost of the liability. For the purposes of this report, the guaranteeing of funds is taken as a sufficient response to the "Polluter Pays Principle". Ethical issues related to the management and disposal of long-lived radioactive waste and to ensuring that future populations are protected at an acceptable level are discussed in other publications [3; 4].

The schemes adopted to guarantee the availability of funds, that are summarised in Table 6.1 below, differ depending on a number of factors.

Table 6.1 Summary of existing schemes for guaranteeing liability funds [1]

Country	Centralised fund, centralised responsibility	Centralised fund, decentralised responsibilities	Guarantees, decentralised responsibilities	Decentralised responsibilities
Australia			√ [2]	
Belgium	√			√ [3]
Canada			√ [2]	√
Finland		√		
France				√
Germany				√
Italy	√			
Japan				√
Korea	√ [4]			√ [3]
Netherlands				√
Spain	√			
Sweden		√		
Switzerland				√
Turkey				√
UK				√
US	√ [4; 5]		√ [3]	

1. In NEA countries which provided information.
2. For mines only.
3. For decommissioning (and spent fuel management in Belgium).
4. For long-lived waste.
5. For enrichment plants.

For example, different schemes are adopted whether the fund is centrally controlled (generally by the State) or not and whether technical responsibility for the management of the liabilities also rests with a central body. In some cases, a distinction is made between liabilities resulting from decommissioning and from waste management. In certain countries, the schemes may also differ depending on the source of liability and on the companies involved. Therefore, the categorisation given in this chapter should be considered a guide for understanding the various systems rather than a rigid division of approaches. Other schemes may certainly be considered and implemented.

6.1 Centralised control of funds, centralised responsibility for the liability

Spain is the most typical example of centralised control with regard to liabilities. All liabilities related to decommissioning and waste and the control of the fund for taking care of the liabilities rest with one company, ENRESA, which gets its revenue from an electricity levy (see section 5.3.2). A Royal decree obliges ENRESA to present annually to the Ministry of Industry and Energy a "General Radioactive Waste Plan" (GRWP) which shall include the revision of all necessary actions and applicable technical solutions during the expected time of radioactive waste activity, including the economic and financial study of the costs of those actions. ENRESA has taken responsibility for all nuclear activities, including decommissioning of old yellow cake mills, except for remedial actions related to mining and milling which rest with ENUSA.

In **Belgium,** the National Agency for Radioactive Waste and Enriched Fissile Materials ONDRAF/NIRAS is in charge of managing all radioactive waste on Belgian territory, regardless of its origin and source. It is responsible for all R & D needed to carry out its mandate. Its funding comes from two sources. On the one hand, producers pay, at the time of waste delivery, the full cost of all necessary management steps, raw waste handling and conditioning (when applicable), transportation and interim storage of conditioned waste awaiting disposal, for which no site is presently available in Belgium. At the same time, provisions are paid to the so-called "Long-Term Fund" which is legally required to cover all liabilities related to final disposal of the waste. In all cases, the payments or provisions are determined in order to minimise the risk of having insufficient financial means when needed.

On the other hand, waste management related historic liabilities (pre-1989), decommissioning and site restoration are funded by special agreements between the Belgian State and the electricity sector.

Funds administered by ONDRAF/NIRAS are under the supervision of a board of representatives from the State and the main waste generators involved. The board monitors cash flows and the portfolio of investments.

In the **United States**, under the Nuclear Waste Policy Act, nuclear utilities pay 1 mill per kWh of nuclear electricity generated into the Nuclear Waste Fund in order to fund the Department of Energy's programmes for final disposition of high-level waste, in this case, spent fuel. Funding for liabilities related to enrichment plants comes from a Federal fund, similar to the one for high-level waste. The Secretary of the Treasury collects a special assessment from domestic utilities, and appropriations complete the yearly deposits into the fund. There are periodic reviews and updates of the funds required as well as of the adequacy of the funding mechanism and contributions. Decommissioning responsibility rests with the owners/operators of the facilities.

In **Korea** waste management is the responsibility of NEMAC, a subsidiary of KAERI. Money for waste management is paid by generators of radioactive waste into a waste management fund controlled by the government as the government is responsible for final waste disposal. The fund is invested into national or public bonds as well as into bank accounts. However, KEPCO, the State-owned utility, is responsible for decommissioning and, therefore, accumulates funds to cover decommissioning, spent fuel and radioactive waste disposal and puts them aside into an in-house fund which is reinvested into the company.

6.2 Centralised control of funds, decentralised responsibility for the liability

This covers schemes where the waste producers are responsible for all management and disposal operations as well as the financing. However the funds accumulated for these liabilities are kept in a separate centralised account, usually under direct government control. Schemes in Sweden and Finland fall into this category.

In **Finland,** holders of licences for nuclear technology activities are responsible for the management of all types of waste (spent fuel, low- and intermediate-level waste and decommissioning waste), as well as all management measures (R & D, handling, conditioning, storage, transportation, decommissioning and final disposal). The State has provided all assets needed to cover liabilities of a research reactor.

If the costs of the waste management are estimated to exceed FIM200 000 (about US$40 000) the assets must be collected in advance in a separate fund. The Ministry of Trade and Industry determines yearly the amount of the liability and the fund contribution. The liability and the fund contribution are defined for each nuclear waste producer. The fund is arranged such that the fund's assets match the expected liabilities. Non-recurrent costs, such as are the decommissioning costs and investments for disposal facilities, can be distributed over no more than the first 25 operating years of the power plants. Therefore the fund assets will not match the liability during the early years of operation. To compensate for this, the waste producer shall furnish securities to cover the outstanding liabilities. At present, the securities are in the form of non-nuclear related real estate of the nuclear power utilities or in the form of guarantees from the owner of the utilities. The assets, plus the securities, must cover the total liabilities.

The fund invests the assets through loans and the interest collected is credited to the account of the waste producer. The waste producer has the right to borrow up to 75 per cent of his own contribution backed by normal commercial guarantees. The State may borrow the remaining 25 per cent. If the rights are not exercised, the fund lends on the open market. According to this system, which is continuously updated, all waste management measures and activities are covered and paid for by the originator of the liability.

Sweden has a very similar system. The holder of a licence for nuclear activities is responsible for ensuring the safe handling and final storage of nuclear waste and the safe shutting down and demolishing of plants which gave rise to the waste. The licence holder is also responsible for all R & D necessary to conduct these tasks.

A fee system has been set up which is based on the energy produced from power plants. The fee is calculated based on the operational life of the reactor (25 years is assumed) and other factors that may influence the liability. SKB, a company jointly owned by the reactor operators, prepares an estimate of the future costs of managing nuclear waste and spent fuel and for decommissioning, and submits a plan to SKI every year. A contingency allowance of about 27 per cent is included. After having evaluated the costs, SKI propose to the government the fees to be paid for the next year.

The money is deposited in an interest-bearing account in the National Bank. From the accumulated funds, the State makes reimbursements to the nuclear power utilities to cover any costs they may have for their current waste management activities. A recently appointed commission has proposed some modification to the Act to include guarantees by the reactor owners for the difference between accumulated funds and future commitments, should the funds prove insufficient. The commission also proposed setting up a special organisation to manage the funds with a more liberal investment policy and therefore a higher rate of return.

The Swedish system differs from the Finnish one only in the management of the fund's assets. Guarantees are not presently demanded to compensate for assets not covering the liability at the start of the reactor life. An amendment to the Financing Act is expected to request guarantees similar to the Finnish system.

6.3 Guarantees, decentralised responsibility for the liability

In this category fall other schemes where the producer of the liability maintains responsibility for the liability and the funds, though the funds may not be under its direct control. However some sort of guarantee, legal, contractual or otherwise, is in place.

In the **United States**, the Atomic Energy Act requires the owner/operator of a nuclear facility to decommission the facility at the end of its life, and to take responsibility for accumulating funds to cover this liability.

Each licensee (operator or owner of a nuclear facility), as a condition of its licence, must maintain funds to cover these liabilities (apart from high-level waste), and these are reviewed annually. Under certain conditions, licensees may self fund. However, in most cases licensees maintain a decommissioning fund. This applies to all licensees even in the case where the ownership is governmental such as TVA or other municipal electric utilities. Four types of funds are acceptable to the NRC:

- An external fund that builds up over the lifetime of the facility.

- A prepayment account which is kept separately from the owner's other assets and is outside its control.

- A surety bond, letter of credit or insurance which guarantees that decommissioning costs will be paid if the utility defaults on its obligation. Or

- Corporate self-guarantee based on certain financial criteria such as a net worth of more than US$1 000 million, a net worth at least ten times the decommissioning costs, 90 per cent of its assets in the United States and a bond rating of at least A, and absence of control of the voting stock by a parent company. This method is not available to electric utilities.

In **Australia**, the guarantees for liabilities arising from uranium mining activities are contractual. There are three mines permitted to export uranium from Australia: Ranger, Nabarlek in the Northern Territory and Olympic Dam in South Australia. Regulation of mining is the responsibility of individual States. Therefore, the level of security varies and is dependent on the normal system of laws and regulations covering commercial practices in the different States. In 1995, the Commonwealth Government introduced a minimum cash (Australian $30 million) and balance by unconditional bank garantee.

The Ranger mine has responsibility for rehabilitation. By contract with the State the company must provide an amount equivalent to the assessed cost of rehabilitation plus a contingency (not exceeding 10 per cent) as security. The funds are held in a trust fund. The State is considering an option to permit a minimum cash balance with the remainder provided by unconditional bank guarantees. Nabarlek does not need to provide any plan for rehabilitation or financial security with the

Northern Territory (NT) against non-compliance with rehabilitation requirements. However the NT has requested and received a decommissioning proposal and a guarantee (Australian $10 million) from the parent company. The company, by contract with the Aboriginal community, is required to provide an Australian $1 million security against failure to rehabilitate. For Olympic Dam a plan for rehabilitation must be provided. There is no provision of a security for rehabilitation.

In **Canada,** the AECB issued regulations in 1994 requiring owner/operators or proponents of uranium and thorium mines to provide financial assurances for the decommissioning of their facilities. The province of Saskatchewan has begun to require similar guarantees for all mining activities in that province.

6.4 Provisions, decentralised responsibility for the liability

In many countries, due to the size of the utilities and ancillary companies or their ownership (see chapter 3), responsibility for the liability and control of the fund rests with large companies. Most countries have funding arrangements which fall in this category.

In **France**, whether for decommissioning or for mine rehabilitation, organisations generating the liability are responsible for both the technical and financial aspects. Cogema, EDF and the CEA present three different aspects of the nuclear activities. In addition to these three bodies, a State agency, ANDRA, is responsible for final disposal of waste and is paid by the producers of the waste (essentially EDF, Cogema and the CEA). Its financial viability is therefore dependent on the three companies noted above.

In the case of Cogema, either part of the decommissioning costs is included in the price charged to the client for services, or the contracts with the clients stipulate that a share of the decommissioning cost will be paid by the customer at the appropriate time. In the first case, moneys are invested in a diversified range of large publicly quoted companies whose shares are freely traded. As the government still owns 89 per cent of Cogema, the State is an implicit guarantor that adequate funds will be available.

With regard to nuclear power plants, the price of electricity includes provisions for future liabilities, and EDF, the FrenchState-owned utility, reinvests the money collected for these liabilities back into EDF. Availability of funds in the future is based upon the realistic assumption that electricity generation and sale will continue to raise sufficient cash flows to finance liabilities when the need will arise.

The CEA is a State-owned organisation dedicated to research. Under the Contract of Objectives for civil activities, agreed between the State and the CEA for 1995-1998, it is noted that proposals will be made to the government to cover the costs not already falling to EDF and Cogema for management of historic waste and decommissioning facilities that are no longer used.

Korea, for decommissioning, and **Belgium**, for decommissioning and spent fuel management, follow similar procedures to those adopted in France by EDF.

The situation of utilities in **Canada** is similar to EDF. Utilities with nuclear power plants are responsible for all the liabilities associated with their operation. The cost of the liabilities is factored into the electricity price and the sums collected are reinvested in normal operation. There is no guarantee apart from the implicit assurance provided by the assets of the utility. Note that the utilities are owned by the provincial government and this offers an additional assurance. Mines are privately owned but follow similar schemes as the utilities. No funds are accumulated in the case of fuel cycle facilities, radioisotope production facilities nor in the case of government owned research facilities.

In the **Netherlands** there is a centralised organisation charged with waste management, COVRA. While the State owns only 10 per cent of COVRA (ECN owns 30 per cent, and the utilities 60 per cent), it maintains control over the funding. The money set aside for future liabilities is normally reinvested into the companies. ECN is an isotope producer and a research centre which invests part of its fund into bonds.

In **Switzerland**, the provisions set aside by the operators are administered by a commission apointed by the Federal Council (Conseil fédéral) and constituted by representatives from the operators and the State. The commission has established regulations for the management of the funds that ensure secure investments, a fair interest rate and adequate liquidity. The management of the funds has been delegated to a third party.

In the **United Kingdom**, where the owners are subject to the legislation governing the conduct of companies, they must follow accepted accounting standards in the preparation of their annual accounts. Those standards require companies to recognise future liabilities and make provision for them in their accounts. Those accounts, including the provisions, must be audited by independent auditors. There are no specific government requirements applying to the management of nuclear liabilities.

The accumulation of funds is represented by the balance sheets of the companies (utilities, BNFL for fuel cycle activities, or Amersham for radioisotope production) as a whole. Funds are reinvested in the business in the form of capital projects, and any excess funds are set aside in the form of gilt or other deposits. These are not nuclear liability specific. Investing funds back into the business means that they are working for the companies and giving a better rate of return than if they were invested in financial instruments. This assumes that the companies will generate the required rate of return from their assets, and that they continue to operate into the future. A review of *"The Prospects for Nuclear Power in the UK"* took place during 1994 and 1995. The conclusions of the review were published in a government White Paper on 9 May 1995. One of the main conclusions was that the more modern parts of the UK nuclear generating industry should be privatised. In the context of this study, it is important to note the review's conclusion that segregated funds were the best way of ensuring public confidence that the parts of Nuclear Electric and Scottish Nuclear which are privatised will meet their obligations. At the time of preparing this report no detail was available of how this conclusion would be implemented.

In certain instances the government has accepted financial responsibility for nuclear liabilities arising from programmes of work undertaken for government. The majority of the nuclear liabilities of the United Kingdom Atomic Energy Authority have been accepted by government in this way, and are funded by government on an annual basis. UKAEA now consists of two elements, a government division with the remit of managing the liabilities for which government has accepted financial responsibility, and AEA Technology, with a remit of selling research, technical and consultant services. Legislation to privatise AEA Technology is expected to complete its passage through Parliament in 1995. All of the nuclear liabilities of the UKAEA remain with the government division, which will remain in the public sector. The government provides the amounts to discharge its liabilities as part of its ordinary expenditure. Some of the liabilities of BNFL, which relate to government nuclear programmes, are funded in a similar way.

The task of developing disposal facilities for intermediate and some low-level waste in the United Kingdom has been placed on Nirex, a private company owned by BNFL, Nuclear Electric, Scottish Nuclear and the UKAEA. The funds required for development are provided by the shareholders, and may in some ways be considered as pre-payment of that part of their liabilities which relate to the disposal of the waste which Nirex will handle.

In **Germany** and **Japan**, responsibility for waste management and decommissioning rests basically with the operators. Japanese utilities and fuel cycle companies reinvest the funds set aside for decommissioning and waste management back into normal operation. As in most other countries research establishments do not set aside funds but rely on government appropriations to cover the liability as the need arises. Isotope production facilities do not set aside funds.

Turkey has no specific requirements for control of funding of future liabilities since nuclear activities are essentially limited to R & D and under the responsibility ofState-owned organisations.

7. CONCLUDING REMARKS, FINDINGS AND RECOMMENDATIONS

Nuclear power plants provide about 17 per cent of electricity production world-wide, contributing almost 6 per cent of the world's primary energy needs. In 1994, for the NEA countries, nuclear electricity production represented 24.4 per cent of total electricity generation. The radioisotopes produced from reactors and laboratories have seen wide beneficial applications in medicine, teaching, research, agriculture, and industries such as chemical, mining, pulp and paper, to name but a few. Also, as is the case for most industrial activities, nuclear activities generate liabilities that need to be adequately addressed. Radioactive waste generated by nuclear facilities requires disposal, and contaminated facilities require decommissioning after the end of their useful life.

Although the public debate tends to be more active in relation to liabilities of the nuclear industry, it should be stressed that creation of such liabilities is not unique to nuclear facilities; some non-nuclear industries which deal with hazardous and toxic materials face similar problems. While the values of the future liabilities generated by these sectors of industry are generally smaller, relative to their incomes, and the lead times for decommissioning of facilities and disposal of waste are generally shorter than for the nuclear industry, some of the principles, concepts and practices, that are already in place in the nuclear industry and are described in this report, might find applications in the non-nuclear sectors.

All sectors of the nuclear industry generate future liabilities, with a need for payments to be made for the operations to be conducted at some relatively distant future period in order to manage and dispose of waste products and to decommission facilities. Recognising the long lead times between the commissioning of nuclear facilities, which generate revenues during their operation, and the payment of liabilities that they have generated, the industry and governments have taken measures ensuring that funding will be available for radioactive waste disposal and decommissioning even if the activities which generated the liabilities would not be producing revenues by that time.

There are three main underlying principles that are respected for nuclear liabilities in the countries reviewed:

1) the polluter pays, i.e. present beneficiaries, should pay for any liabilities caused;
2) all liabilities should be identified and reported;
3) there should be mechanisms to ensure that funds are available to meet the liabilities.

There is an ethical and political need to ensure that the general "Polluter Pays Principle" should operate. A wide interpretation of this principle requires that in addition to minimising and coping with any immediate current pollution, the people who benefit from the provision of the electricity or other commodity, service or product should share the burden of paying for the future liabilities. This applies to both private sector and State-owned companies in the electricity, nuclear fuel cycle and radioisotope production sectors. In the R & D sector, in so far as it has been conducted by State-owned organisations, there has generally been a practice to pay for the waste management and disposal, and decommissioning, out of current government revenues.

The nature and timing of nuclear facility decommissioning and radioactive waste disposal inevitably lead to uncertainties in the amounts of money required for financing future liabilities. Although the principles to be respected and the necessary methods of scientific and technical assessment in this regard are well documented, in particular in a number of NEA and IAEA publications, not all countries have yet defined the standards by which the adequacy of waste disposal will be judged. Few have a complete concept of all the facilities and operations necessary for the safe final disposal of waste. Therefore, mechanisms have been put in place to ensure that the value of liabilities is regularly reviewed and, when necessary, revised, taking into account the progress made in estimating the costs of decommissioning nuclear facilities and disposal of radioactive waste.

According to the information provided by Member countries, the amounts required to cover the future liabilities of the nuclear generating sector, taking account of the whole fuel cycle, are estimated not to be large in comparison with the overall income in the industries concerned and amount to only a few percent of the overall levelised electricity generating cost. In aggregate, however, the liabilities represent very large sums of money.

The problem of providing funds for these end-of-use operations has been recognised for some time in all NEA countries. There is a wide variety of mechanisms used for ensuring that the liabilities are comprehensively identified and reported, that the desired funds are accumulated from beneficiaries of nuclear operations, and that the funds are protected and made available when needed. In some countries there is special tax treatment of the reserves in order not to create a disincentive to responsible behaviour by a company needing to set up a reserve fund.

In the private sector, paying for liabilities when necessary can lead to considerable financial difficulties if the necessary provisions are not made in a timely manner. Under accounting procedures in place in NEA countries, therefore, there is pressure to build up appropriate reserves, funds or provisions in order that companies should continue to be solvent.

The need for special treatment of "historic" liabilities has been recognised by most governments, i.e. where there is no legal successor to a generator of a liability, or where the policy and legal framework at the time of creation of the liability did not provide for the accumulation of adequate funds, or where the liability arises from work by or for government, the government will assume the responsibility for funding the close-out operations. In this regard, there are increasingly widespread measures to ensure that there will be no more "historic" liabilities, as all potential generators of liabilities are called upon to create the necessary financial reserves as from the start of operations.

A variety of funding schemes is currently in use in NEA countries. These range from dependence on normal accounting practice in large diversified companies, to the establishment of a fund administered by a State organisation, built up according to its view of future needs for money, and used by it to carry out the waste disposal and decommissioning operations. Among intermediate variations already in place, funds might be accrued, at a rate determined by a government body, administered by a non-government body separated from the generator of the liability, and spent by the generator whenever necessary.

International studies of schemes for managing future liabilities provide benefits in taking advantage of the experience acquired in order to analyse the extent to which the generally supported principles are reflected in the varying national organisations and contexts.

Transparency in building up the funds is especially relevant in order to strengthen public acceptance of nuclear activities through demonstrating that the full cost of nuclear activities is reflected in the price paid by consumers and that financial mechanisms are in place to cover future liabilities whenever they occur. In particular, in some countries, there is a tendency over time to demand that liability funds are more clearly separated from the overall funds used by the organisations that create the liabilities.

While the "Polluter Pays Principle" requires that consumers should bear the full costs of the products and commodities that they use, including future liabilities, the importance of mechanisms to ensure the availability of funds when the actual expenditures occur highly depends on expectations regarding the future existence, and ability to earn revenues, of the organisations which generate these liabilities.

In the electricity power sector, where the future liabilities are probably the highest and the lead times the longest, this might not be considered a key issue, since electricity is likely to remain an essential service into the indefinite future and, therefore, utilities are likely to continue to exist, even if they were to rely upon different energy mixes in the long term. Therefore there is a possibility of reaching an equilibrium state in which the payment for the close-out operations related to present activities would be equal to the generation of new liabilities in the then current programmes. Nevertheless, the establishment of appropriate provisions or guarantees remains a relevant precaution. On the other side, for non-power nuclear activities, i.e. radioisotope production, it might be more important to adopt special measures to ensure the availability of adequate funds in the long term since market forces are likely to have a greater influence on the future of this sector.

In all NEA countries, the State has retained jurisdiction over the development, use and control of nuclear energy. In the event that the waste generator fails to fulfil its future obligations, the State, in the interest of the public, may be forced into assuming the residual responsibility for the liability. The internationally agreed principles for the management of radioactive waste also provide a basis to establish adequate legal and regulatory frameworks within which the waste generators can fulfil their obligations. In view of these considerations the State should promote:

- the implementation of appropriate mechanisms requiring generators of waste and other nuclear liabilities to assure and, if necessary guarantee, the availability of funds;

- the appropriate evaluation of funds to ensure that they will be sufficient at all times until the relevant liabilities are discharged.

Although there is general awareness and recognition by the industrial operators that future liabilities must be met, States should promote the establishment of a comprehensive system that facilitates fair and consistent application of relevant policies; such systems and arrangements may be different for organisations that are State-owned or State-funded than for those that are not.

Research and development in the field of radioactive waste management and disposal and decommissioning of nuclear facilities should be encouraged as it will reduce the uncertainties related to the cost of future liabilities. Mechanisms should be in place to reflect the progress of scientific and technical know-how in the estimation of future liabilities and the funding set aside for covering them.

8. REFERENCES

1.   *Nuclear Energy Data*, ("Brown Book"), OECD/NEA, 1995.

2.   *Past Trends and the Current State of Nuclear Research Institutes*, OECD/NEA, 1996.

3.   *Environmental and Ethical Aspects of Long-lived Radioactive Waste Disposal, Proceedings of an International Workshop (Paris 1-2 September 1994)*, OECD/NEA, 1995.

4.   *The Environmental and Ethical Basis of Geological Disposal, A Collective Opinion of the NEA Radioactive Waste Management Committee*, OECD/NEA, 1995.

5.   *The Principles of Radioactive Waste Management,, A Publication within the RADWASS Programme, Safety Series No. 111-F*, IAEA, 1995.

6.   *Liability and Compensation for Nuclear Damage, An International Overview*, OECD/NEA, 1994.

7.   *Projected Costs of Generating Electricity, Update 1992*, OECD/NEA-IEA, 1993.

8.   *Decommissioning Policies for Nuclear Facilities, Proceedings of an International Seminar (Paris, 2-4 October 1991)*, OECD/NEA, 1992.

9.   *The Cost of High-level Waste Disposal in Geologic Repositories, An Analysis of Factors Affecting Cost Estimates*, OECD/NEA, 1993.

10. *The Economics of the Nuclear Fuel Cycle*, OECD/NEA, 1994.

11. *Uranium 1993, Resources, Production and Demand*, OECD/NEA, 1994.

12. *Radioactive Waste management: An IAEA Source Book*, IAEA, 1993.

Annex 1

COUNTRY DATA

1. Introduction

This Annex provides specific data and information on NEA Member countries which answered the questionnaire. While the content of the annex is essentially extracted from the country answers to the questionnaire, the format adopted in the tables and graphs has led to some simplifications. Although an effort has been made to be comprehensive, some of the information contained in the country submissions could not be included for the sake of homogeneity across countries and simplicity of presentation. On the other hand, the Secretariat has included additional published data, whenever relevant and necessary, in particular for completing the tables on nuclear activities.

For each country, the annex includes:

- a table on nuclear activities generating liabilities;
- a graph showing the expected schedule of expenses in connection with liabilities; and
- a note on specific issues in the country, whenever relevant.

The table on nuclear activities generating liabilities gives an overview, for each country, on the sectors and main companies/organisations involved but does not intend to provide an exhaustive list of all operators within the national nuclear industry. The type of liabilities and responsibilities is indicated briefly for each company, organisation or sector.

The types of liabilities indicated correspond to the classification adopted in Table 2.1 of the report on "Nature of future liabilities in NEA countries", that is:

a) Reprocessing;

b) Disposal of spent fuel;

c) Disposal of other high-level waste;

d) Disposal of low and intermediate waste;

e) Decommissioning of facilities and/or reclamation of mines.

Five types of responsibilities are identified in the tables:

1) Provision of funds

2) Management of funds;

3) Decommissioning;

4) Reprocessing, when applicable;

5) Waste management and disposal.

The graphs show the scheduled disbursement of provisions for liabilities, according to the indicative information provided by each country as of mid-1994.

AUSTRALIA

NUCLEAR ACTIVITIES

MINING & MILLING

Company	Capacity (tU/y)	Ownership	Type of Liabilities*	Responsibilities*
TOTAL	4,194			
ERA (Ranger)	2,544	Private	} d; e	1; 3
Western Mining Corp.	1,650	Private	}	1; 2; 3

RESEARCH CENTRES

Company/Organisation	Ownership	Type of Liabilities*	Responsibilities*
ANSTO	State owned	} b, d: e	2; 3
Australian Radiation Laboratory	State owned	}	

ISOTOPE PRODUCTION

Company/Organisation	Ownership	Type of Liabilities*	Responsibilities*
ANSTO	State owned	d; e	2; 3

WASTE DISPOSAL

Company	Type of Waste	Capacity	Ownership	Type of Liabilities*	Responsibilities*
State agencies	LLW/ILW		State owned	e	5

*   See explanatory notes in section 1: Introduction.

ANSTO: Australian Nuclear Science and Technology Organisation
ERA: Energy Resources of Australia Ltd.

AUSTRALIA

INDICATIVE SCHEDULED DISBURSEMENT OF PROVISIONS FOR LIABILITIES

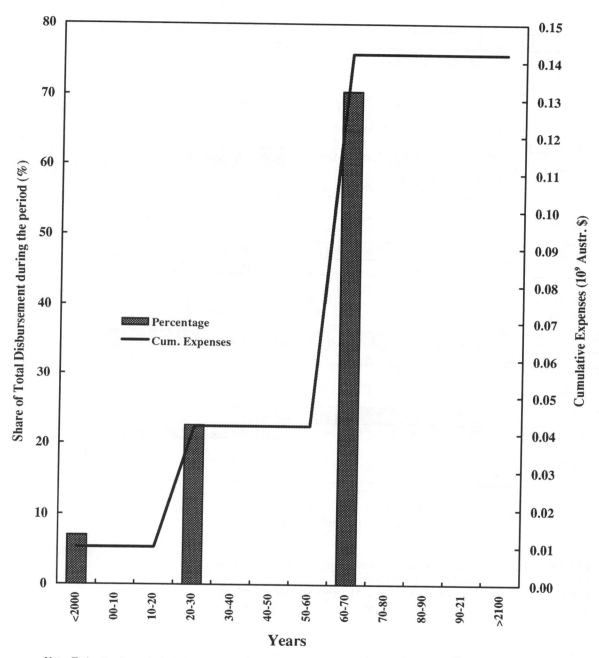

Note: Estimates do not include costs of rehabilitation of the Olympic Dam multi-minerals mining operation beyond 2100, nor costs associated with the disposal of spent fuel, low and intermediate wastes or any replacement reactor for the high flux reactor HIFAR.

BELGIUM

NUCLEAR ACTIVITIES

FUEL CYCLE

Sector	Company	Capacity	Ownership	Type of Liabilities*	Responsibilities*
Fabrication	FBFC	400 tU(LWR)/y	Private	d; e	1; 2**; 3
	Belgonucleaire	35 tMOX/y	50% State owned	c; d; e	1; 2**; 3
Fuel Management	Synatom	120 t spent fuel/y	Private	a; b; c; d	1; 2; 4

NUCLEAR POWER PLANTS (as of 1/1/95)

	Units	Nucl. Cap. (GWe)	Nucl. Gen. (TWh)	Nucl. Share (%)	Ownership	Type of Liabilities*	Responsibilities*
Electrabel	7	5.5	38.2	55.8	Private	d; e	1; 2**; 3

RESEARCH CENTRES

Company/Organisation	Ownership	Type of Liabilities*	Responsibilities*
SCK/CEN IRMM	State owned (Federal) European Commission	} d; e }	1; 2**; 3

ISOTOPE PRODUCTION

Company/Organisation	Ownership	Type of Liabilities*	Responsibilities*
IRE	State owned	d; e	1; 3

WASTE DISPOSAL

Company	Type of Waste	Capacity	Ownership	Type of Liabilities*	Responsibilities*
ONDRAF/NIRAS	LLW/ILW		State owned (Federal)	e***	1; 2; 3; 5

*   See explanatory notes in Section 1: Introduction.
**   With regard to provision for decommissioning of own facilities.
***   And historic waste.

FBFC International: Société Franco-Belge de Fabrication de Combustibles
IRE: Institut des Radioéléments
IRMM: Institute for Reference Materials and Measurements
SCK/CEN: Studiecentrum voor Kernenergie/Centre d'Etudes Nucléaires

BELGIUM

INDICATIVE SCHEDULED DISBURSEMENT OF PROVISIONS FOR LIABILITIES

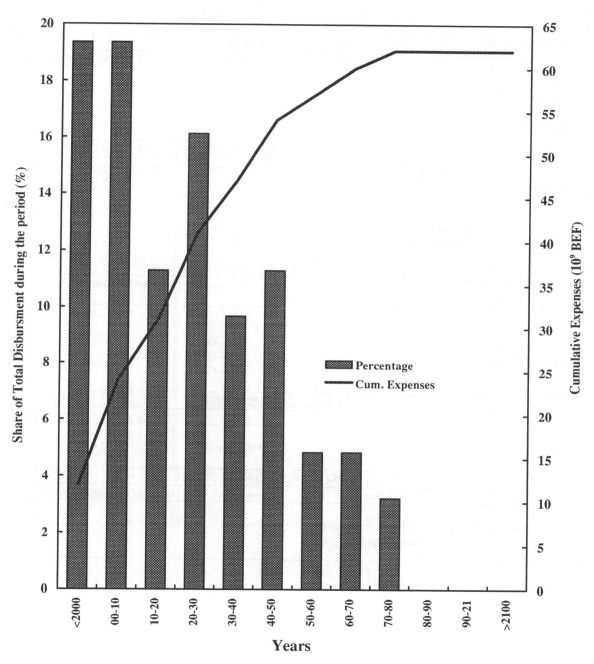

Note: Disbursement schedule for ONDRAF/NIRAS only, taking into account waste management programme for future waste arising as planned in a reference scenario

CANADA

NUCLEAR ACTIVITIES

MINING & MILLING

Company	Capacity (tU/y)	Ownership	Type of Liabilities*	Responsibilities*
TOTAL	15,000			
Cameco		Private	}	
Cogema		Private	} d; e	1; 2; 3; 5
Rio Algom		Private	}	

FUEL CYCLE

Sector	Company	Capacity	Ownership	Type of Liabilities*	Responsibilities*
Conversion	Cameco	2,500 tUO$_2$/y	Private	}	
		10,500 tUF$_6$/y		}	
				} d; e	1; 2; 3; 5
Fabrication	Zircatec Prec. Ind.	} Total	Private	}	
	Can. Gen. Elec.	} 2 500 fuel bdl/y	Private	}	

NUCLEAR POWER PLANTS (as of 1/1/95)

	Units	Nucl. Cap. (GWe)	Nucl. Gen. (TWh)	Nucl. Share (%)	Ownership	Type of Liabilities*	Responsibilities*
TOTAL	22	15.4	110.4	13.9			
Ontario Hydro	20	14.8			Prov. Gov.	}	
Hydro Quebec	1	0.6			Prov. Gov.	} b; d; e	1; 2; 3; 5
N. B. Power	1	0.6			Prov. Gov.	}	

RESEARCH CENTRES

Company/Organisation	Ownership	Type of Liabilities*	Responsibilities*
AECL	State owned	b; d; e	1; 2; 3; 5

ISOTOPE PRODUCTION

Company	Activities	Ownership	Type of Liabilities*	Responsibilities*
Nordion International	Manufac. & marketing of radioisotopes	Private	d; e	1; 2; 3; 5

* See explanatory notes in section 1: Introduction.

CANADA

INDICATIVE SCHEDULED DISBURSEMENT OF PROVISIONS FOR LIABILITIES

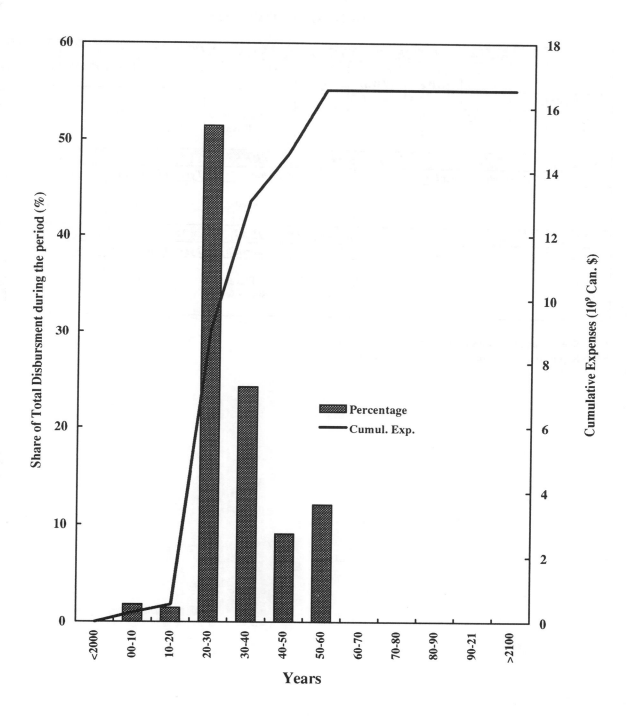

FINLAND

<table>
<tr><td colspan="7" align="center">**NUCLEAR ACTIVITIES**</td></tr>
<tr><td colspan="7" align="center">*NUCLEAR POWER PLANTS (as of 1/1/95)*</td></tr>
<tr><td></td><td>*Units*</td><td>*Nucl. Cap. (GWe)*</td><td>*Nucl. Gen. (TWh)*</td><td>*Nucl. Share (%)*</td><td>*Ownership*</td><td>*Type of Liabilities**</td><td>*Responsibilities**</td></tr>
<tr><td>**TOTAL**</td><td>4</td><td>2.3</td><td>18.3</td><td>29.5</td><td></td><td></td><td></td></tr>
<tr><td>IVO</td><td>2</td><td>0.9</td><td></td><td></td><td>State owned</td><td>}   **b; d; e**</td><td rowspan="2">**1; 3; 5**</td></tr>
<tr><td>TVO</td><td>2</td><td>1.4</td><td></td><td></td><td>Private</td><td>}</td></tr>
</table>

RESEARCH CENTRES			
Company/Organisation	*Ownership*	*Type of Liabilities**	*Responsibilities**
VTT	Sate owned	**b; d; e**	**1; 3; 5**

WASTE DISPOSAL					
Company	*Type of Waste*	*Capacity*	*Ownership*	*Type of Liabilities**	*Responsibilities**
TVO	LLW/ILW	8,800 m³	Private	e	5
IVO**	LLW/ILW	5,500 m³	State owned	e	5

*   See explanatory notes in Section 1: Introduction.
**   Repository under construction, to be in operation in 1997.

FINLAND

INDICATIVE SCHEDULED DISBURSEMENT OF PROVISIONS FOR LIABILITIES

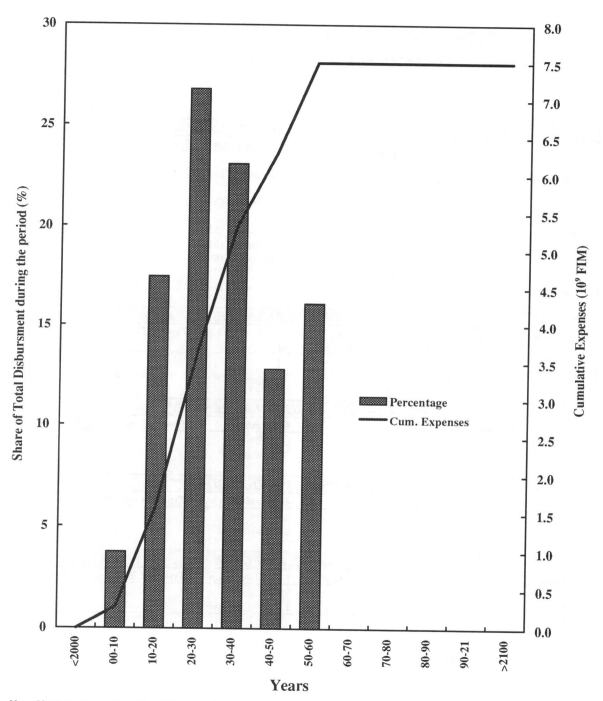

Note: Not including 1,500 million FIM spent for waste management before 2000

FRANCE

NUCLEAR ACTIVITIES				

MINING & MILLING

Company	Capacity (tU/y)	Ownership	Type of Liabilities*	Responsibilities*
Cogema & subsidiaries	1,570	State Owned (89%)	d; e	1; 2; 3

FUEL CYCLE

Sector	Company	Capacity	Ownership	Type of Liabilities*	Responsibilities*
Conversion	Comhurex	14,000 tU/y	State owned (89%)	d; e	1; 2; 3
Enrichment	Eurodif	10,500 tSWU/y	State owned (Maj.)	d; e	1; 2; 3
Fabrication	FBFC International	1,150 tHM(LWR)/y	State owned (Maj.)	c; d; e	1; 2; 3
	MELOX	135 tMOX/y	State owned (Maj.)	c; d; e	1; 2; 3
	Cogema	30 tHM/y	State owned (89%)	c; d; e	1; 2; 3
Reprocessing	Cogema	1,600 tHM/y	State owned (89%)	c; d; e	1; 2; 3; 4

NUCLEAR POWER PLANTS (as of 1/1/95)

Company	Units	Nucl. Cap. (GWe)	Nucl. Gen. (TWh)	Nucl. Share (%)	Ownership	Type of Liabilities*	Responsibilities*
EDF	56	58.5	342	75	State owned	a; c; d; e	1; 2; 3

RESEARCH CENTRES

Company/Organisation	Ownership	Type of Liabilities*	Responsibilities*
CEA	State owned	c; d; e	3

ISOTOPE PRODUCTION

Company/Organisation	Ownership	Type of Liabilities*	Responsibilities*
CEA	State owned	d; e	3

WASTE DISPOSAL

Company	Type of Waste	Capacity	Ownership	Type of Liabilities*	Responsibilities*
ANDRA	LLW/ILW	1.5 10^6 m^3	State owned	e	5

* See explanatory notes in Section 1: Introduction.
FBFC International: Société Franco-Belge de Fabrication de Combustibles.

FRANCE

INDICATIVE SCHEDULED DISBURSEMENT OF PROVISIONS FOR LIABILITIES

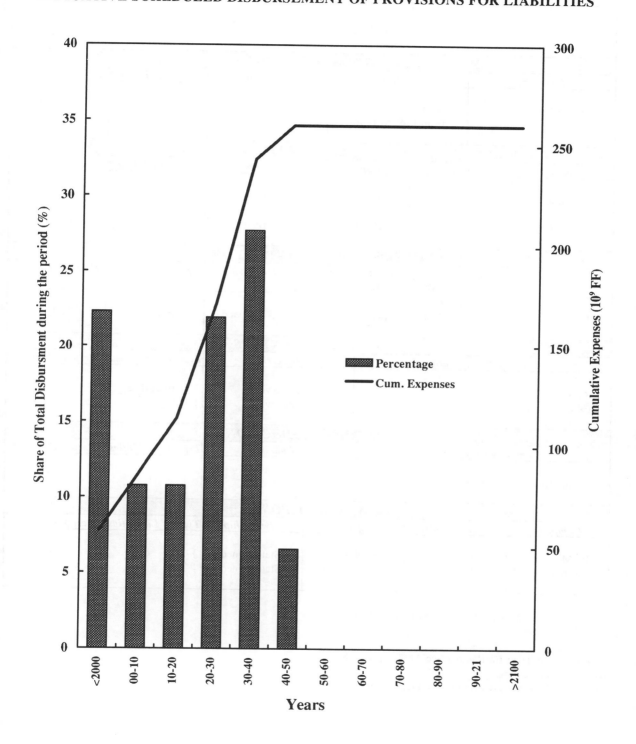

GERMANY

NUCLEAR ACTIVITIES

MINING & MILLING

Company	Capacity (tU/y)	Ownership	Type of Liabilities*	Responsibilities*
Wismut GmbH	[200,000 tU produced from 1946 to 1990]	State owned	d; e	3; 5

FUEL CYCLE

Sector	Company	Capacity	Ownership	Type of Liabilities*	Responsibilities*
Enrichment	Urenco	1 000 tSWU/y	Private	d; e	1; 2; 3
Fabrication	Siemens	950 tHM/y	Private	d; e	1; 2; 3

NUCLEAR POWER PLANTS (as of 1/1/95)

	Units	Nucl. Cap. (GWe)	Nucl. Gen. (TWh)	Nucl. Share (%)	Ownership	Type of Liabilities*	Responsibilities*
TOTAL	21	22.6	142.9	29.3	All private	a; b; d; e	1; 2; 3

RESEARCH CENTRES

Company/Organisation	Ownership	Type of Liabilities*	Responsibilities*
KFA	State owned	} b; c; d; e	3; 5
FZK	State owned	}	

ISOTOPE PRODUCTION

Company/Organisation	Ownership	Type of Liabilities*	Responsibilities*
No information available			

WASTE DISPOSAL

Company	Type of Waste	Capacity	Ownership	Type of Liabilities*	Responsibilities*
ERAM	LLW/ILW	5 000 m³/y	State owned	} e	5
Schacht Konrad**	LLW/ILW	16 000 m³/y	State owned	}	

*   See explanatory notes in section 1: Introduction.
**   Being licensed.

ERAM: Endlager für Radioaktive Abfälle Morsleben
KFA: Forschungzentrum Jülich
FZK: Forschungzentrum Karlsruhe; formerly KfK

GERMANY

INDICATIVE SCHEDULED DISBURSEMENT OF PROVISIONS FOR LIABILITIES

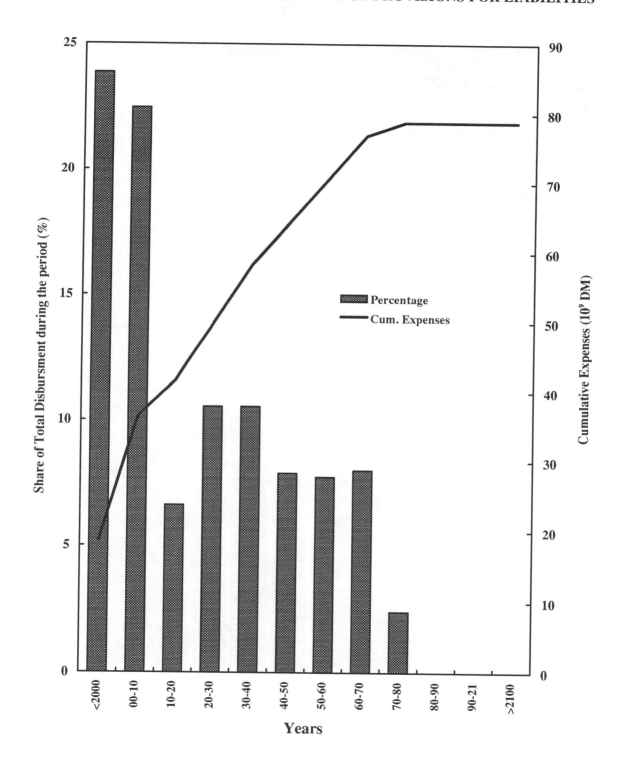

ITALY

NUCLEAR ACTIVITIES							
NUCLEAR POWER PLANTS (as of 1/1/95)							
Company	*Units*	*Nucl. Cap. (GWe)*	*Nucl. Gen. (TWh)*	*Nucl. Share (%)*	*Ownership*	*Type of Liabilities**	*Responsibilities**
ENEL	4	1.5**	0	0	State owned***	**b; c; d; e**	**1; 2; 3; 4; 5**

*   See explanatory notes in Section 1: Introduction.

**   During operation, i.e. before 1987.

***   Sale of company's share anticipated in 1995/96.

ITALY

INDICATIVE SCHEDULED DISBURSEMENT OF PROVISIONS FOR LIABILITIES

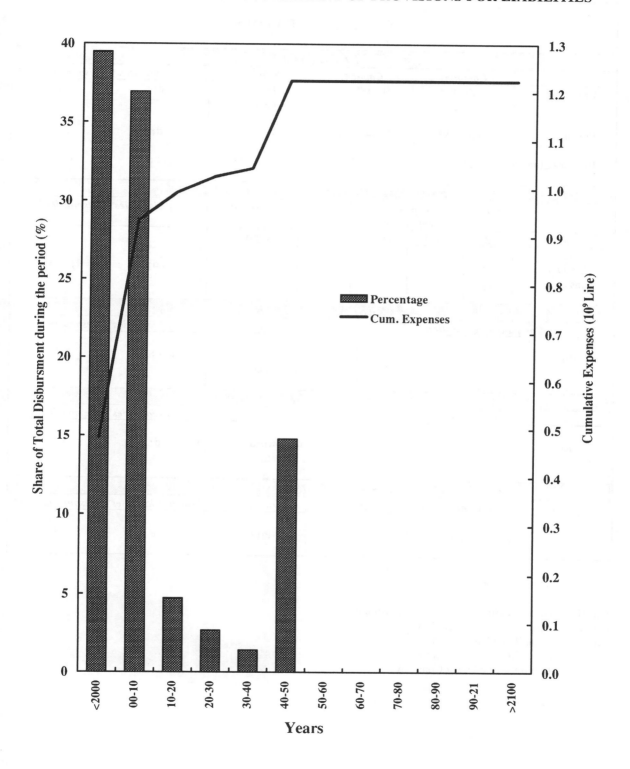

JAPAN

NUCLEAR ACTIVITIES

FUEL CYCLE

Sector	Company	Capacity	Ownership	Type of Liabilities*	Responsibilities*
Enrichment	JNFL	600 tSWU/y	Private	} d; e	3.5
	PNC	200 tSWU/y	State owned	}	
Fabrication	Total (LWR)	1,714 tHM/y	Private	d; e	3; 5
Reprocessing	PNC	0.7 tHM/y	State owned	c; d; e	3; 4; 5

NUCLEAR POWER PLANTS (as of 1/1/95)

	Units	Nucl. Cap. (GWe)	Nucl. Gen. (TWh)	Nucl. Share (%)	Ownership	Type of Liabilities*	Responsibilities*
TOTAL	48	40.4	264.9	31.3	All private	}	
Including						} a; d; e	1; 2; 3; 5
TEPCO	15					}	
Kansai	11					}	

RESEARCH CENTRES

Company/Organisation	Ownership	Type of Liabilities*	Responsibilities*
JAERI	State owned	} a; c; d; e	3;4;5
PNC	State owned	}	

ISOTOPE PRODUCTION

Company/Organisation	Ownership	Type of Liabilities*	Responsibilities*
JAERI	State owned	} d; e	3; 5
JRIA	Private	}	

WASTE DISPOSAL

Company	Type of Waste	Capacity	Ownership	Type of Liabilities*	Responsibilities*
JNFL	LLW	40,000 m^3	Private	e	5

*   See explanatory notes in section 1: Introduction.

JAERI: Japan Atomic Energy Research Institute
JNFL: Japan Nuclear Fuel Co. Ltd.
JRIA: Japan Radio Isotope Association
PNC: Power Reactor & Nuclear Fuel Co.
TEPCO: Tokyo Electric Power Company

JAPAN

INDICATIVE SCHEDULED DISBURSEMENT OF PROVISIONS FOR LIABILITIES

Provisions for financing the future financial liabilities associated with reprocessing of spent fuel and decommissioning of nuclear power plants are accumulated by utilities. At the end of FY (fiscal year) 1993, the funds accumulated amounted to 1,302 thousand million yen for reprocessing and 439 thousand million yen for decommissioning of nuclear power plants. The funds will be disbursed in accordance with arising costs.

Although the overall policy for addressing liability issues has been set up, concrete procedures and plans for storage and disposal of high-level waste and the associated cost estimates have not yet been established.

KOREA

<table>
<tr><th colspan="6">NUCLEAR ACTIVITIES</th></tr>
<tr><th colspan="6">FUEL CYCLE</th></tr>
<tr><th>Sector</th><th>Company</th><th>Capacity</th><th>Ownership</th><th>Type of Liabilities*</th><th>Responsibilities*</th></tr>
<tr><td>Conversion</td><td>KAERI</td><td>100 tU/y</td><td>State owned</td><td>d; e</td><td>1; 2; 3</td></tr>
<tr><td>Fabrication</td><td>KNF
KAERI</td><td>200 tHM(LWR)/y
100 tHM(HWR)/y</td><td>State owned
State owned</td><td>} d; e
}</td><td>1; 2; 3</td></tr>
</table>

<table>
<tr><th colspan="7">NUCLEAR POWER PLANTS (as of 1/1/95)</th></tr>
<tr><th></th><th>Units</th><th>Nucl. Cap. (GWe)</th><th>Nucl. Gen. (TWh)</th><th>Nucl. Share (%)</th><th>Ownership</th><th>Type of Liabilities*</th><th>Responsibilities*</th></tr>
<tr><td>KEPCO</td><td>9</td><td>7.6</td><td>58.6</td><td>35.5</td><td>State owned</td><td>b; c; d; e</td><td>1; 2; 3</td></tr>
</table>

<table>
<tr><th colspan="4">RESEARCH CENTRES</th></tr>
<tr><th>Company/Organisation</th><th>Ownership</th><th>Type of Liabilities*</th><th>Responsibilities*</th></tr>
<tr><td>KAERI</td><td>State owned</td><td>c; d; e</td><td>1; 2; 3</td></tr>
</table>

<table>
<tr><th colspan="4">ISOTOPE PRODUCTION</th></tr>
<tr><th>Company/Organisation</th><th>Ownership</th><th>Type of Liabilities*</th><th>Responsibilities*</th></tr>
<tr><td>KAERI</td><td>State owned</td><td>d; e</td><td>1; 2; 3</td></tr>
</table>

<table>
<tr><th colspan="6">WASTE DISPOSAL</th></tr>
<tr><th>Company</th><th>Type of Waste</th><th>Capacity</th><th>Ownership</th><th>Type of Liabilities*</th><th>Responsibilities*</th></tr>
<tr><td>NEMAC</td><td>LLW/ILW/HLW</td><td></td><td>State owned</td><td>e</td><td>5</td></tr>
</table>

*　　See explanatory notes in Section 1: Introduction.

KNF:　　Korea Nuclear Fuel Corporation Ltd.

KOREA

INDICATIVE SCHEDULED DISBURSEMENT OF PROVISIONS FOR LIABILITIES

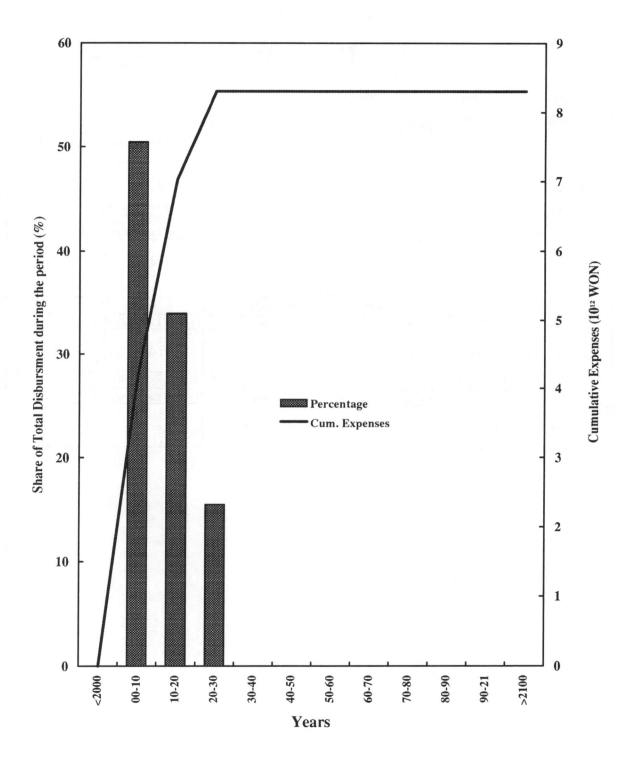

NETHERLANDS

<table>
<tr><td colspan="6" align="center">NUCLEAR ACTIVITIES</td></tr>
<tr><td colspan="6" align="center">FUEL CYCLE</td></tr>
<tr><td>Sector</td><td>Company</td><td>Capacity</td><td>Ownership</td><td>Type of Liabilities*</td><td>Responsibilities*</td></tr>
<tr><td>Enrichment</td><td>Urenco</td><td>1,300 tSWU/y</td><td>Private</td><td>d; e</td><td>1; 2; 3</td></tr>
</table>

	Units	Nucl. Cap. (GWe)	Nucl. Gen. (TWh)	Nucl. Share (%)	Ownership	Type of Liabilities*	Responsibilities*

NUCLEAR POWER PLANTS (as of 1/1/95)

	Units	Nucl. Cap. (GWe)	Nucl. Gen. (TWh)	Nucl. Share (%)	Ownership	Type of Liabilities*	Responsibilities*
TOTAL	2	0.5	3.7	5.4	All private	a; c; d; e	1; 2; 3

RESEARCH CENTRES

Company/Organisation	Ownership	Type of Liabilities*	Responsibilities*
ECN	Foundation; less than 50% of the budget coming from the government	c; d; e	1; 2; 3

ISOTOPE PRODUCTION

Company	Activities	Ownership	Type of Liabilities*	Responsibilities*
Mallinckrodt Medical	Prod. of medical isotopes	Private	c; d; e	1; 2; 3

WASTE DISPOSAL

Company	Type of Waste	Capacity	Ownership	Type of Liabilities*	Responsibilities*
COVRA	LLW/ILW/HLW		Private	b; c; d; e	1;5

*   See explanatory notes in section 1: Introduction.

NETHERLANDS

INDICATIVE SCHEDULED DISBURSEMENT OF PROVISIONS FOR LIABILITIES

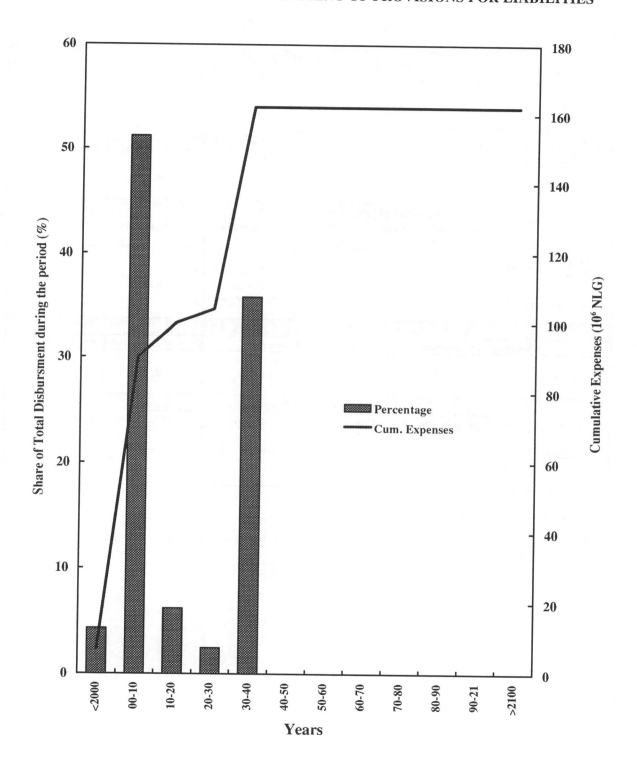

SPAIN

NUCLEAR ACTIVITIES

MINING & MILLING

Company	Capacity (tU/y)	Ownership	Type of Liabilities*	Responsibilities*
ENUSA	255	State owned	e	1;2;3

FUEL CYCLE

Sector	Company	Capacity	Ownership	Type of Liabilities*	Responsibilities*
Fabrication	ENUSA		State owned	d; e	1

NUCLEAR POWER PLANTS (as of 1/1/95)

	Units	Nucl. Cap. (GWe)	Nucl. Gen. (TWh)	Nucl. Share (%)	Ownership	Type of Liabilities*	Responsibilities*
TOTAL	9	7.4	53	35			
Iberdrola					Private }		
Union Fenosa					Private }	b; d; e	1
Endesa Group					State owned (maj.) }		

RESEARCH CENTRES

Company/Organisation	Ownership	Type of Liabilities*	Responsibilities*
CIEMAT	State owned	d; e	3

WASTE DISPOSAL

Company	Type of Waste	Capacity	Ownership	Type of Liabilities*	Responsibilities*
ENRESA	LLW/ILW HLW	(as of 1/1/95) 3,000 m³ 0	State owned	e	2;3;5

* See explanatory notes in section 1: Introduction.

CIEMAT: Centro de Investigation Energetica, Medioambiental y Tecnologica (Centre for Energy, Environmental and Technological Research)

SPAIN

INDICATIVE SCHEDULED DISBURSEMENT OF PROVISIONS FOR LIABILITIES

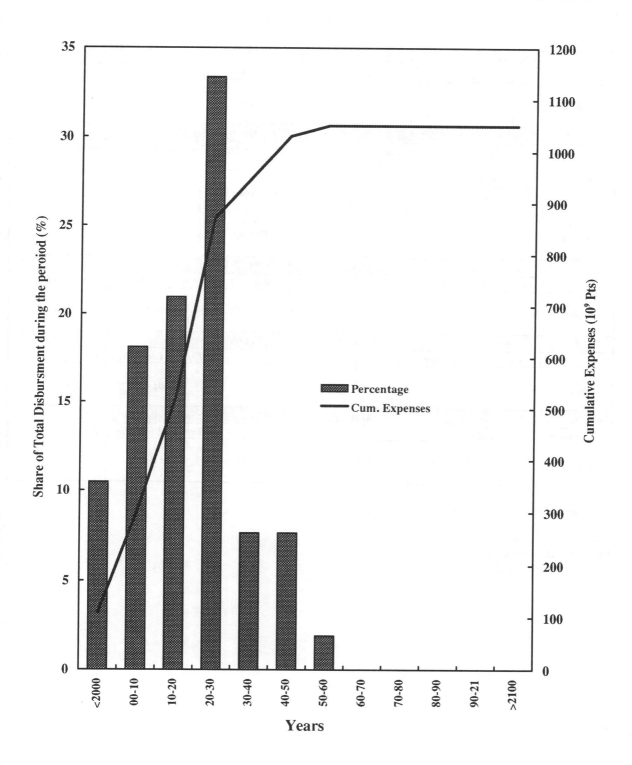

SWEDEN

NUCLEAR ACTIVITIES

FUEL CYCLE

Sector	Company	Capacity	Ownership	Type of Liabilities*	Responsibilities*
Fabrication	ABB	400 tHM/y	Private	e	3

NUCLEAR POWER PLANTS (as of 1/1/95)

	Units	Nucl. Cap. (GWe)	Nucl. Gen. (TWh)	Nucl. Share (%)	Ownership	Type of Liabilities*	Responsibilities*
TOTAL	12	10.0	68.2	51.0			
Vattenfall	4	3.5			State owned }		
Forsmark K.	3	3.1			State owned ((maj.) }	b; d; e	1; 3; 5
OKG	3	2.2			Private }		
BK AB	2	1.2			Private }		

RESEARCH CENTRES

Company/Organisation	Ownership	Type of Liabilities*	Responsibilities*
Studsvik AB	Private	d; e	1; 3; 5

ISOTOPE PRODUCTION

Company/Organisation	Ownership	Type of Liabilities*	Responsibilities*
Studsvik AB	Private	d; 3	1; 3; 5

WASTE DISPOSAL

Company	Type of Waste	Capacity	Ownership	Type of Liabilities*	Responsibilities*
SKB	LLW/ILW/HLW	90,000 m³	Private	b; d; e	3; 5

*   See explanatory notes in section 1: Introduction.

ABB: Asea Brown Bovery
BK AB: Barsebeck AB
OKG: OKG Aktiebolag

INDICATIVE SCHEDULED DISBURSEMENT OF PROVISIONS FOR LIABILITIES

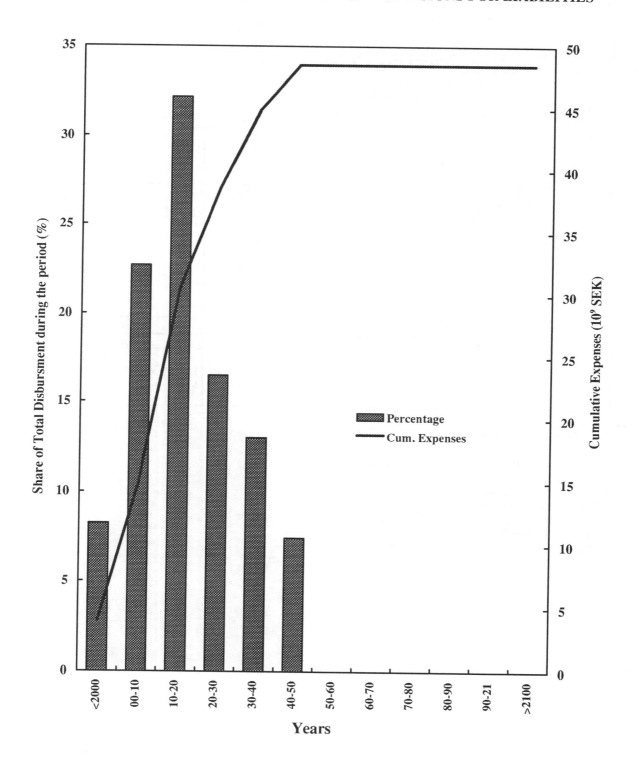

SWITZERLAND

NUCLEAR ACTIVITIES

NUCLEAR POWER PLANTS (as of 1/1/95)

	Units	Nucl. Cap. (GWe)	Nucl. Gen. (TWh)	Nucl. Share (%)	Ownership	Type of Liabilities*	Responsibilities*
TOTAL	5	3.1	23.0	36.1			
NOK	2	0.7			**	}	
KKL	1	1.0			***	} a; b; d; e	1; 2; 3
KKG	1	1.0			***	}	
BKW	1	0.4			**	}	

RESEARCH CENTRES

Company/Organisation	Ownership	Type of Liabilities*	Responsibilities*
Paul Scherrer Institute	State owned	}	
Ecole Polytechnique de Lausanne	State owned	} d; e	1; 2; 3
CERN	International Research Facility partly located in Switzerland	}	

WASTE DISPOSAL

Company	Type of Waste	Capacity	Ownership	Type of Liabilities*	Responsibilities*
NAGRA	LLW/ILW/HLW		NPP owners/State	} e	5
GWN	LLW		NPP owners	}	

---

*   See explanatory notes in section 1: Introduction.
**   Owned by municipalities and cantons.
***   Owned by private, cantons and municipalities.

NOK: Nordostschweizerische Kraftwerke AG
KKL: Kern Kraftwerk Leibstadt
KKG: Kern Kraftwerk Goesgen-Daeniken AG
BKW: Bernische Kraftwerke AG
CERN: Centre Européen de Recherche Nucléaire
NAGRA: National cooperative for the disposal of radioactive waste

INDICATIVE SCHEDULED DISBURSEMENT OF PROVISIONS FOR LIABILITIES

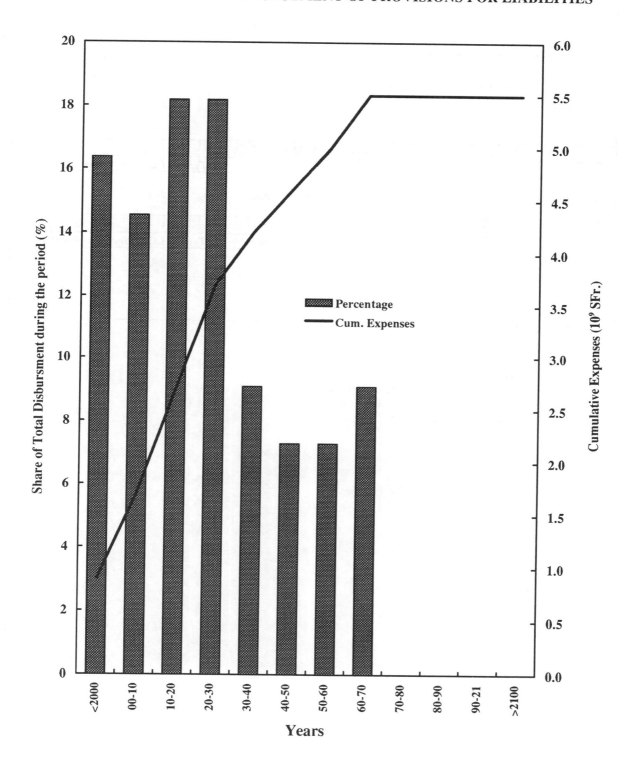

TURKEY

NUCLEAR ACTIVITIES				
RESEARCH CENTRES				
Company/Organisation		*Ownership*	*Type of Liabilities**	*Responsibilities**
ÇNAEM ITU-NEE	} }	State owned	d; e	3
ISOTOPE PRODUCTION				
Company/Organisation		*Ownership*	*Type of Liabilities**	*Responsibilities**
ÇNAEM		State owned	d; e	3
WASTE DISPOSAL				
Company	*Type of Waste*	*Capacity* / *Ownership*	*Type of Liabilities**	*Responsibilities**
TAEK	LLW	2 m³ liquid/week 1-10 drum solid/day total 1 000 drums / State owned	e	5

*   See explanatory notes in section 1: Introduction.

MTA: General Directorate Mineral Research and Exploration
ÇNAEM: Cekmece Nuclear Research and Training Centre
ITU-NEE: Istanbul Technical University-Nuclear Energy Institute
TAEK: Turkish Atomic Energy Authority

TURKEY

INDICATIVE SCHEDULED DISBURSEMENT OF PROVISIONS FOR LIABILITIES

Nuclear activities carried out in Turkey for the time being are essentially in the field of R & D and under the responsibility ofState-owned organisations. There is no established regulation concerning liabilities arising from nuclear activities.

UNITED KINGDOM

NUCLEAR ACTIVITIES

FUEL CYCLE

Sector	Company	Capacity	Ownership	Type of Liabilities*	Responsibilities*
Conversion	BNFL	6,000 tUF6/y	State owned	d; e	1; 2; 3; 5
Enrichment	URENCO	1,150 tSWU/y	Private	d; e	1; 2; 3; 5
Fabrication	BNFL	300 tHM(AGR)/y 300 tHM(PWR)/y 750 tHM(Magn.)/y	State owned	d; e	1; 2; 3; 5
Reprocessing	BNFL	**Magnox fuel** 1,500 tHM/y **Oxide fuel** 7,000 tHM over 10 years 850 tHM/y thereafter	State owned	c; d; e	1; 2; 3; 4; 5

NUCLEAR POWER PLANTS (as of 1/1/95)

	Units	Nucl. Cap. (GWe)	Nucl. Gen. (TWh)	Nucl. Share (%)	Ownership	Type of Liabilities*	Responsibilities*
TOTAL	34	11.9	88.3	27.1			
Nuclear Elec.	22	9.1			State owned }		
Scottish Nuc.	4	2.4			State owned }	a; c; d; e	1; 2; 3; 5
BNFL	8	0.4			State owned }		

RESEARCH CENTRES

Company/Organisation	Ownership	Type of Liabilities*	Responsibilities*
UKAEA	State owned	a; c; d; e	1; 2; 3; 4; 5

ISOTOPE PRODUCTION

Company/Organisation	Ownership	Type of Liabilities*	Responsibilities*
Amersham International	Private	} d; e	1; 2; 3; 5

WASTE DISPOSAL

Company	Type of Waste	Capacity	Ownership	Type of Liabilities*	Responsibilities*
Nirex	ILW		Private (maj.) }		
BNFL	LLW		State owned }	e	3; 5
UKAEA (for its own wastes)	LLW		State owned }		

* See explanatory notes in section 1: Introduction.

UNITED KINGDOM

INDICATIVE SCHEDULED DISBURSEMENT OF PROVISIONS FOR LIABILITIES

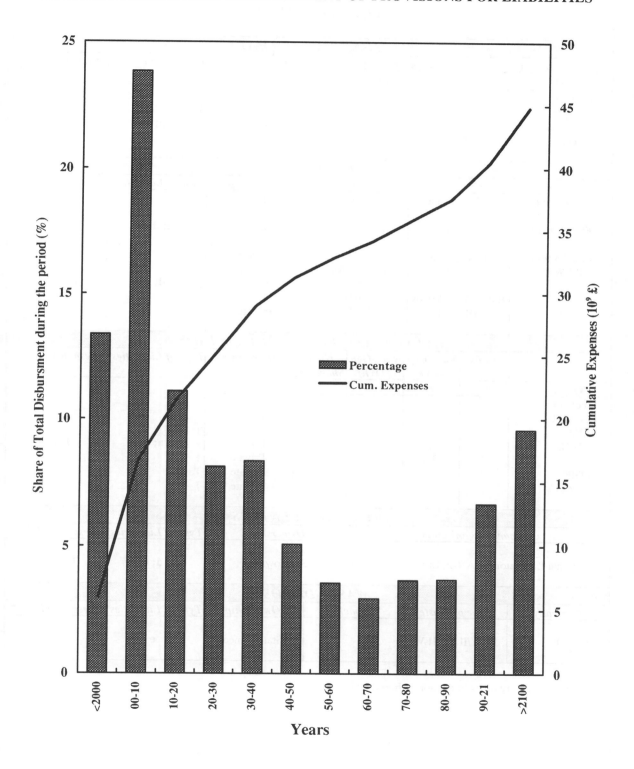

UNITED STATES

NUCLEAR ACTIVITIES

MINING & MILLING

Company	Capacity (tU/y)	Ownership	Type of Liabilities*	Responsibilities*
TOTAL	3,800			
Including: Malapai Crow Butte Freeport		Private Private Private	} } d; e }	1; 2; 3

FUEL CYCLE

Sector	Company	Capacity	Ownership	Type of Liabilities*	Responsibilities*
Conversion	Allied-Signal	12,700 tUF6/y	Private	d; e	1; 2; 3; 5
Enrichment	USEC	1,150 tSWU/y	State owned	c; d; e	1; 2; 3; 5
Fabrication (all LWR)	Westinghouse Gen. Elec. Siemens Babcock & Wilcox ABB C-E	1,150 tHM/y 1,100 tHM/y 700 tHM/y 400 tHM/y 300 tHM/y	Private Private Private Private Private	} } } d; e } }	1; 2; 3; 5

NUCLEAR POWER PLANTS (as of 1/1/95)

	Units	Nucl. Cap. (GWe)	Nucl. Gen. (TWh)	Nucl. Share (%)	Ownership	Type of Liabilities*	Responsibilities*
TOTAL	109	99	639	19.6			
Including: COMED TVA DUKE APS PGEC VYNPC	 12 5 7 3 2 1	 11.7 6.2 4.8 3.8 1.2 0.5			 Private State owned Private Private Private Private	} } } a; d; e } } }	1; 2; 3

RESEARCH CENTRES

Company/Organisation	Ownership	Type of Liabilities*	Responsibilities*
National Laboratories (ANL; LLL, ...)	State owned	d; e	1; 2; 3; 5

WASTE DISPOSAL

Company	Type of Waste	Capacity	Ownership	Type of Liabilities*	Responsibilities*
USDOE	LLW/ILW/HLW		State owned	e	3; 5

*   See explanatory notes in Section 1: Introduction.

UNITED STATES

INDICATIVE SCHEDULED DISBURSEMENT OF PROVISIONS FOR LIABILITIES

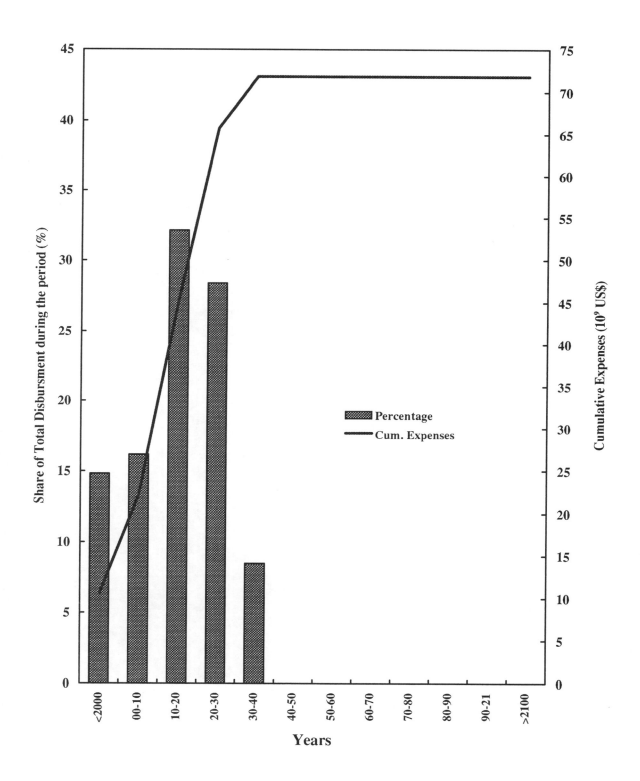

LIST OF ABBREVIATIONS AND GLOSSARY OF TERMS

AECB

Atomic Energy Control Board (Canada)

AECL

Atomic Energy of Canada Limited

ANDRA

Agence Nationale pour la gestion des Déchets Radioactifs (National agency for radioactive waste management, France)

Assessment, performance

An analysis to predict the performance of a system or subsystem, followed by comparison of the results of such analysis with appropriate standards or criteria. A performance assessment becomes a safety assessment when the system under consideration is the overall waste disposal system and the performance measure is radiological impact or some other global measure of impact on safety. Performance assessment can be used to describe the analysis and comparison of systems at a variety of levels and requirements.

Assessment, safety

An analysis to predict the performance of an overall system and its impact, where the performance measure is radiological impact or some other global measure of impact on safety. (See also assessment, performance.)

Barrier

A physical obstruction that prevents or delays the movement (for example, migration) of radionuclides or other material between components in a system, for example, a waste repository. In general, a barrier can be either an engineered barrier or a natural barrier which is inherent to the environment of the repository.

Barriers, multiple

Two or more barriers. (See barrier.)

BfS

Bundesamt für Sthrahlenschutz (Federal bureau for radioprotection, Germany)

BMU

BundesMinisterium für Umwelt, Naturschutz und Reaktorsicherheit (Federal Ministry for environment, protection of nature and nuclear safety, Germany)

BNFL

British Nuclear Fuels plc

CEA

Commissariat à l'Energie Atomique (Atomic Energy Commission, France)

Closure (permanent)

The term closure refers to the status of or an action directed at a disposal facility at the end of its operating life. A disposal facility is placed into permanent closure usually after completion of waste emplacement, by covering for a near surface disposal facility, by backfilling and/or sealing of a geological repository and the passages leading to it, and termination and completion of activities in any associated structures.

COGEMA

Compagnie Générale des Matières nucléaires (Company for nuclear material and fuel-cycle service supply, France)

Commingled tailings

Commingled tailings are tailings that resulted from the mixing of waste produced under contacts with the US Government and tailings from commercial production contracts

COVRA

Centrale Organisatie Voor Radioactief Afval (Central organisation for radioactive waste, Netherlands)

DBE

Deutsche Gessellschaft für Bau und Betrieb von Endlagern für Abfallstoffe mbH (Company responsible for the construction of radioactive waste repositories, Germany)

DOE

Department of Energy (of the United States)

Disposal

The emplacement of waste in an approved, specified facility (for example, near surface or geologic repository) without the intention of retrieval. Disposal may also include the approved direct discharge of effluents (for example, liquid and gaseous waste) into the environment with subsequent dispersion.

EC

European Commission

ECN

Energieonderzoerk Centrum Nederland (Energy research centre, Netherlands)

EDF

Electricité de France (Electric utility, France)

ENEL

Ente Nazionale per l'Energia Elettrica (Electric utility, Italy)

ENRESA

Empresa Nacional de Residuos Radioactivos (National Waste Management Company, Spain)

ENUSA

Empresa Nacional del Uranio (National Uranium Company, Spain)

Fuel, spent (used)

Irradiated fuel not intended for further use in its current form.

Fuel cycle (nuclear)

Sequence of processes connected with nuclear reactor operation, including the mining and milling of fissile materials, enrichment, fabrication, utilisation and storage of nuclear fuel, optional reprocessing of spent fuel, and processing and disposal of resulting waste.

GNS

Gessellschaft für Nuklear-Service (Company that takes care of all radioactive waste and spent fuel management obligations, Germany)

GRWP

General Radioactive Waste Plan (Spain)

HLW

High-level Waste

HM

Heavy metal

IAEA

International Atomic Energy Agency

ILW

Intermediate-level Waste

Institutional control

Control of a waste site (for example, disposal site, decommissioning site, etc.) by an authority or institution designated under the laws of a country or State. This control may be active (monitoring, surveillance, remedial work) or passive (land use control) and may be a factor in the design of a nuclear facility (for example, near surface disposal facility).

IVO

Imatran Voima Oy (Power Company, Finland)

JET

Joint European Torus

KAERI

Korea Atomic Energy Research Institute

KEPCO
> Korea Electric Power Company

Licence
> A formal, legally prescribed document issued by the regulatory body to perform specified activities related to the siting, design, construction, commissioning, operation, decommissioning of a nuclear facility, closure of a disposal facility, close-out of a mining and mill tailings site, or institutional control. A licence may be specific (i.e. issued to an individual person or entity) or general (i.e. issued to a class of persons or activities).

LLRWMO
> Low-level Radioactive Waste Management Office (Canada)

LLW
> Low-level Waste

LMR
> Liquid metal reactor

Long term
> In radioactive waste disposal, refers to periods of time which exceed the time during which active institutional control can be expected to last.

LWR
> Light-water reactor

Monitoring
> The measurement of radiological or non-radiological parameters for reasons related to the assessment or control of exposure and the interpretation of such measurements. Monitoring can be continuous or non-continuous.

MOX
> Mixed oxide (U/Pu) fuel

NDC
> Nuclear Development Committee (OECD/NEA)

NEMAC
> Nuclear Environment Centre (Korea)

NPP
> Nuclear power plant

NPV
> Net Present Value

NT
> Northern Territories (Australia)

NRC

Nuclear Regulatory Commission (United States)

Nuclear facility

A facility and its associated land, buildings and equipment in which radioactive materials are produced, processed, used, handled, stored or disposed of (for example, repository) on such a scale that consideration of safety is required.

NVGKN

N.V. Gemeenschappelijke Kernenergiecentrale Nederland (Dodewaard nuclear power plant, Netherlands)

ONDRAF/NIRAS

Organisme National des Déchets Radioactifs et des Matières Fissiles Enrichies (National organisation for radioactive waste and enriched fissile materials, Belgium)

Operator (or operating organisation)

The organisation (and its contractors) which performs activities to select and investigate the suitability of a site for a nuclear facility, and/or undertakes to design, construct, commission, operate and decommission such a facility. This term is preferred to "implementing organisation" which appeared in earlier literature.

Regulatory body

An authority or a system of authorities designated by the government of a State as having legal authority for conducting the regulatory process, including issuing licences or authorisations, and thereby for regulating the sitting, design, construction, commissioning, operation, closure, close-out, decommissioning and, if required, subsequent institutional control of the nuclear facilities (for example, near surface repository) or specific aspects thereof. Such authority may be an existing organisation in the field of nuclear related health and safety, mining safety or environmental protection, which is empowered with the appropriate legal authority.

Repository

A nuclear facility (for example, geological repository) where waste is placed for disposal. Future retrieval of waste from the repository is not intended. (See also disposal and nuclear facility).

Repository, geological

A nuclear facility for waste disposal located underground (usually more than several hundred metres below the surface) in a stable geological formation to provide long-term isolation of radionuclides from the biosphere. Usually such a repository would be used for long lived and/or high-level waste.

R & D

Research and Development

SFR

Swedish Final repository

SKB

Svensk Kärnbränlehantering A. B. (Nuclear fuel and waste management company, Sweden)

SKI

Statens Kärnkraftinspecktion (Nuclear power inspectorate, Sweden)

TVA

Tennessee Valley Authority (Electric utility, United States)

TVO

Teollisuuden Voima Oy (Power Company, Finland)

UKAEA

United Kingdom Atomic Energy Authority

USEC

United States Enrichment Corporation

VTT

Technical Research Centre of Finland

VYR

The Finnish State Nuclear Waste Management Fund

Waste, disposal

Emplacement of waste in an approved, specified facility without the intention of retrieval. Disposal may also include the approved direct discharge of effluents, e.g. liquid and gaseous waste, into the environment with subsequent dispersion.

Waste, high-level

High-level waste include:

a) radioactive liquid containing most of the fission products and actinides originally present in spent fuel and forming the residue from the first solvent extraction cycle in reprocessing and some of the associate waste streams;

b) solidified high-level waste from a) above and spent fuel (if it is declared a waste);

c) any other waste with an activity level comparable to a) or b).

High-level waste in practice is considered long lived. One of the characteristics which distinguishes high-level waste from less active waste is its level of thermal power.

Waste, long lived

Radioactive waste containing long lived radionuclides having sufficient radio-toxicity in quantities and/or concentrations requiring long-term isolation from the biosphere. The term "long-lived radionuclide" refers to half-lives usually greater than 30 years.

Waste, low and intermediate level

Radioactive waste in which the concentration of or quantity of radionuclides is above clearance levels established by the regulatory body, but with a radionuclide content and thermal power below those of high-level waste. Low and intermediate-level waste is often separated into short lived and long lived waste. Short lived waste may be disposed of in near surface disposal facilities, whereas long lived waste are planned to be disposed of in geological repositories.

Waste management

All activities, administrative and operational, that are involved in the handling, treatment, conditioning, transportation and disposal of waste.

Waste, radioactive

For legal and regulatory purposes, radioactive waste may be defined as material that contains or is contaminated with radionuclides at concentrations or activities greater than clearance levels as established by the regulatory body, and for which no use is foreseen. (It should be recognised that this definition is purely for regulatory purposes, and that material with activity concentrations equal to or less than clearance levels is radioactive from a physical viewpoint - although the associated radiological hazards are considered negligible.)

Waste, short lived

Radioactive waste which will decay to a level which is considered to be insignificant from a radiological view point in a time period during which institutional control can be expected to last. Radionuclides in short lived waste will generally have half-lives shorter than 30 years (See also waste, long lived.)

Waste form

The waste in its physical and chemical form after treatment and/or conditioning (resulting in a solid product) prior to packaging. The waste form is a component of the waste package.

Waste generator

The operating organisation of the facility where the waste is generated. (See also operator.)

Waste package

The product of conditioning that includes the waste form and any container(s) and internal barriers (for example, absorbing materials and liner), as prepared in accordance with requirements for handling, transportation, storage and/or disposal.

LIST OF MEMBERS OF THE EXPERT GROUP

BELGIUM	Mr. J. DELVOYE	TRACTEBEL
	Mr. D. EMMERY	ONDRAF/NIRAS
	Mr. P. KUNSCH	ONDRAF/NIRAS
	Mr. P. HAVARD	ELECTRABEL
CANADA	Mr. P. L. DE (**Chairman**)	LLRWMO
FINLAND	Ms. S. VILKAMO	Ministry of Trade & Industry
FRANCE	M. J. - F. GERVAIS (**Principal Author**)	COGEMA
	M. D. MEREY	CEA
	M. J. RIVIER	EDF
GERMANY	Mr. R. PAPP	FZK
JAPAN	Mr. H. HOTTA	MITI
	Mr. H. MORIMOTO	MITI
KOREA	Mr. Ki-Gap PARK	Department of Law, Hallym University
NETHERLANDS	Mr. R. SLANGE	Ministry of Economic Affairs
SPAIN	Mr. J. - L. GONZALEZ GOMEZ (**Principal Author**)	ENRESA
SWEDEN	Mr. M. ERIKSSON	Swedish Nuclear Power Inspectorate
	Mr. J. KARLBERG	Swedish Radiation Protection Institute
TURKEY	Mr. M. MENDILCIOGLU	Min. of Energy & Natural Resources
U K	Mr. P. HUBBARD	Department of Trade and Industry
	Mr. A. BLEEZE	Health and Safety Executive
EC	M. M. BARAZZONI	DG XVII
IAEA	Mr. L. BENNETT	Division of Nuclear Power
	Mme. E. BERTEL	Division of Nuclear Power
NEA/OECD	Mr. G. STEVENS	Head, Nuclear Development Division
	Mr. P. GIROUARD (**Scientific Secretary**)	Nuclear Development Division

MAIN SALES OUTLETS OF OECD PUBLICATIONS
PRINCIPAUX POINTS DE VENTE DES PUBLICATIONS DE L'OCDE

ARGENTINA – ARGENTINE
Carlos Hirsch S.R.L.
Galería Güemes, Florida 165, 4° Piso
1333 Buenos Aires   Tel. (1) 331.1787 y 331.2391
Telefax: (1) 331.1787

AUSTRALIA – AUSTRALIE
D.A. Information Services
648 Whitehorse Road, P.O.B 163
Mitcham, Victoria 3132   Tel. (03) 9210.7777
Telefax: (03) 9210.7788

AUSTRIA – AUTRICHE
Gerold & Co.
Graben 31
Wien I   Tel. (0222) 533.50.14
Telefax: (0222) 512.47.31.29

BELGIUM – BELGIQUE
Jean De Lannoy
Avenue du Roi 202 Koningslaan
B-1060 Bruxelles   Tel. (02) 538.51.69/538.08.41
Telefax: (02) 538.08.41

CANADA
Renouf Publishing Company Ltd.
1294 Algoma Road
Ottawa, ON K1B 3W8   Tel. (613) 741.4333
Telefax: (613) 741.5439
Stores:
61 Sparks Street
Ottawa, ON K1P 5R1   Tel. (613) 238.8985
12 Adelaide Street West
Toronto, ON M5H 1L6   Tel. (416) 363.3171
Telefax: (416)363.59.63

Les Éditions La Liberté Inc.
3020 Chemin Sainte-Foy
Sainte-Foy, PQ G1X 3V6   Tel. (418) 658.3763
Telefax: (418) 658.3763

Federal Publications Inc.
165 University Avenue, Suite 701
Toronto, ON M5H 3B8   Tel. (416) 860.1611
Telefax: (416) 860.1608

Les Publications Fédérales
1185 Université
Montréal, QC H3B 3A7   Tel. (514) 954.1633
Telefax: (514) 954.1635

CHINA – CHINE
China National Publications Import
Export Corporation (CNPIEC)
16 Gongti E. Road, Chaoyang District
P.O. Box 88 or 50
Beijing 100704 PR   Tel. (01) 506.6688
Telefax: (01) 506.3101

CHINESE TAIPEI – TAIPEI CHINOIS
Good Faith Worldwide Int'l. Co. Ltd.
9th Floor, No. 118, Sec. 2
Chung Hsiao E. Road
Taipei   Tel. (02) 391.7396/391.7397
Telefax: (02) 394.9176

**CZECH REPUBLIC –
RÉPUBLIQUE TCHÈQUE**
Artia Pegas Press Ltd.
Narodni Trida 25
POB 825
111 21 Praha 1   Tel. (2) 242 246 04
Telefax: (2) 242 278 72

DENMARK – DANEMARK
Munksgaard Book and Subscription Service
35, Nørre Søgade, P.O. Box 2148
DK-1016 København K   Tel. (33) 12.85.70
Telefax: (33) 12.93.87

EGYPT – ÉGYPTE
Middle East Observer
41 Sherif Street
Cairo   Tel. 392.6919
Telefax: 360-6804

FINLAND – FINLANDE
Akateeminen Kirjakauppa
Keskuskatu 1, P.O. Box 128
00100 Helsinki
Subscription Services/Agence d'abonnements :
P.O. Box 23
00371 Helsinki   Tel. (358 0) 121 4416
Telefax: (358 0) 121.4450

FRANCE
OECD/OCDE
Mail Orders/Commandes par correspondance :
2, rue André-Pascal
75775 Paris Cedex 16   Tel. (33-1) 45.24.82.00
Telefax: (33-1) 49.10.42.76
Telex: 640048 OCDE
Internet: Compte.PUBSINQ @ oecd.org
Orders via Minitel, France only/
Commandes par Minitel, France exclusivement :
36 15 OCDE
OECD Bookshop/Librairie de l'OCDE :
33, rue Octave-Feuillet
75016 Paris   Tel. (33-1) 45.24.81.81
(33-1) 45.24.81.67

Dawson
B.P. 40
91121 Palaiseau Cedex   Tel. 69.10.47.00
Telefax : 64.54.83.26

Documentation Française
29, quai Voltaire
75007 Paris   Tel. 40.15.70.00

Economica
49, rue Héricart
75015 Paris   Tel. 45.78.12.92
Telefax : 40.58.15.70

Gibert Jeune (Droit-Économie)
6, place Saint-Michel
75006 Paris   Tel. 43.25.91.19

Librairie du Commerce International
10, avenue d'Iéna
75016 Paris   Tel. 40.73.34.60

Librairie Dunod
Université Paris-Dauphine
Place du Maréchal-de-Lattre-de-Tassigny
75016 Paris   Tel. 44.05.40.13

Librairie Lavoisier
11, rue Lavoisier
75008 Paris   Tel. 42.65.39.95

Librairie des Sciences Politiques
30, rue Saint-Guillaume
75007 Paris   Tel. 45.48.36.02

P.U.F.
49, boulevard Saint-Michel
75005 Paris   Tel. 43.25.83.40

Librairie de l'Université
12a, rue Nazareth
13100 Aix-en-Provence   Tel. (16) 42.26.18.08

Documentation Française
165, rue Garibaldi
69003 Lyon   Tel. (16) 78.63.32.23

Librairie Decitre
29, place Bellecour
69002 Lyon   Tel. (16) 72.40.54.54

Librairie Sauramps
Le Triangle
34967 Montpellier Cedex 2   Tel. (16) 67.58.85.15
Tekefax: (16) 67.58.27.36

A la Sorbonne Actual
23, rue de l'Hôtel-des-Postes
06000 Nice   Tel. (16) 93.13.77.75
Telefax: (16) 93.80.75.69

GERMANY – ALLEMAGNE
OECD Publications and Information Centre
August-Bebel-Allee 6
D-53175 Bonn   Tel. (0228) 959.120
Telefax: (0228) 959.12.17

GREECE – GRÈCE
Librairie Kauffmann
Mavrokordatou 9
106 78 Athens   Tel. (01) 32.55.321
Telefax: (01) 32.30.320

HONG-KONG
Swindon Book Co. Ltd.
Astoria Bldg. 3F
34 Ashley Road, Tsimshatsui
Kowloon, Hong Kong   Tel. 2376.2062
Telefax: 2376.0685

HUNGARY – HONGRIE
Euro Info Service
Margitsziget, Európa Ház
1138 Budapest   Tel. (1) 111.62.16
Telefax: (1) 111.60.61

ICELAND – ISLANDE
Mál Mog Menning
Laugavegi 18, Pósthólf 392
121 Reykjavik   Tel. (1) 552.4240
Telefax: (1) 562.3523

INDIA – INDE
Oxford Book and Stationery Co.
Scindia House
New Delhi 110001   Tel. (11) 331.5896/5308
Telefax: (11) 332.5993
17 Park Street
Calcutta 700016   Tel. 240832

INDONESIA – INDONÉSIE
Pdii-Lipi
P.O. Box 4298
Jakarta 12042   Tel. (21) 573.34.67
Telefax: (21) 573.34.67

IRELAND – IRLANDE
Government Supplies Agency
Publications Section
4/5 Harcourt Road
Dublin 2   Tel. 661.31.11
Telefax: 475.27.60

ISRAEL – ISRAËL
Praedicta
5 Shatner Street
P.O. Box 34030
Jerusalem 91430   Tel. (2) 52.84.90/1/2
Telefax: (2) 52.84.93

R.O.Y. International
P.O. Box 13056
Tel Aviv 61130   Tel. (3) 546 1423
Telefax: (3) 546 1442

Palestinian Authority/Middle East:
INDEX Information Services
P.O.B. 19502
Jerusalem   Tel. (2) 27.12.19
Telefax: (2) 27.16.34

ITALY – ITALIE
Libreria Commissionaria Sansoni
Via Duca di Calabria 1/1
50125 Firenze   Tel. (055) 64.54.15
Telefax: (055) 64.12.57
Via Bartolini 29
20155 Milano   Tel. (02) 36.50.83

Editrice e Libreria Herder
Piazza Montecitorio 120
00186 Roma   Tel. 679.46.28
Telefax: 678.47.51

Libreria Hoepli
Via Hoepli 5
20121 Milano   Tel. (02) 86.54.46
Telefax: (02) 805.28.86

Libreria Scientifica
Dott. Lucio de Biasio 'Aeiou'
Via Coronelli, 6
20146 Milano   Tel. (02) 48.95.45.52
Telefax: (02) 48.95.45.48

JAPAN – JAPON
OECD Publications and Information Centre
Landic Akasaka Building
2-3-4 Akasaka, Minato-ku
Tokyo 107   Tel. (81.3) 3586.2016
Telefax: (81.3) 3584.7929

KOREA – CORÉE
Kyobo Book Centre Co. Ltd.
P.O. Box 1658, Kwang Hwa Moon
Seoul   Tel. 730.78.91
Telefax: 735.00.30

MALAYSIA – MALAISIE
University of Malaya Bookshop
University of Malaya
P.O. Box 1127, Jalan Pantai Baru
59700 Kuala Lumpur
Malaysia   Tel. 756.5000/756.5425
Telefax: 756.3246

MEXICO – MEXIQUE
OECD Publications and Information Centre
Edificio INFOTEC
Av. San Fernando no. 37
Col. Toriello Guerra
Tlalpan C.P. 14050
Mexico D.F.
    Tel. (525) 606 00 11 Extension 100
Fax : (525) 606 13 07

Revistas y Periodicos Internacionales S.A. de C.V.
Florencia 57 - 1004
Mexico, D.F. 06600   Tel. 207.81.00
Telefax: 208.39.79

NETHERLANDS – PAYS-BAS
SDU Uitgeverij Plantijnstraat
Externe Fondsen
Postbus 20014
2500 EA's-Gravenhage   Tel. (070) 37.89.880
Voor bestellingen: Telefax: (070) 34.75.778

NEW ZEALAND – NOUVELLE-ZÉLANDE
GPLegislation Services
P.O. Box 12418
Thorndon, Wellington   Tel. (04) 496.5655
Telefax: (04) 496.5698

NORWAY – NORVÈGE
NIC INFO A/S
Bertrand Narvesens vei 2
P.O. Box 6512 Etterstad
0606 Oslo 6   Tel. (022) 57.33.00
Telefax: (022) 68.19.01

PAKISTAN
Mirza Book Agency
65 Shahrah Quaid-E-Azam
Lahore 54000   Tel. (42) 353.601
Telefax: (42) 231.730

PHILIPPINE – PHILIPPINES
International Booksource Center Inc.
Rm 179/920 Cityland 10 Condo Tower 2
HV dela Costa Ext cor Valero St.
Makati Metro Manila   Tel. (632) 817 9676
Telefax : (632) 817 1741

POLAND – POLOGNE
Ars Polona
00-950 Warszawa
Krakowskie Przedmieácie 7   Tel. (22) 264760
Telefax : (22) 268673

PORTUGAL
Livraria Portugal
Rua do Carmo 70-74
Apart. 2681
1200 Lisboa   Tel. (01) 347.49.82/5
Telefax: (01) 347.02.64

SINGAPORE – SINGAPOUR
Gower Asia Pacific Pte Ltd.
Golden Wheel Building
41, Kallang Pudding Road, No. 04-03
Singapore 1334   Tel. 741.5166
Telefax: 742.9356

SPAIN – ESPAGNE
Mundi-Prensa Libros S.A.
Castelló 37, Apartado 1223
Madrid 28001   Tel. (91) 431.33.99
Telefax: (91) 575.39.98

Mundi-Prensa Barcelona
Consell de Cent No. 391
08009 – Barcelona   Tel. (93) 488.34.92
Telefax: (93) 487.76.59

Llibreria de la Generalitat
Palau Moja
Rambla dels Estudis, 118
08002 – Barcelona
    (Subscripcions) Tel. (93) 318.80.12
    (Publicacions) Tel. (93) 302.67.23
Telefax: (93) 412.18.54

SRI LANKA
Centre for Policy Research
c/o Colombo Agencies Ltd.
No. 300-304, Galle Road
Colombo 3   Tel. (1) 574240, 573551-2
Telefax: (1) 575394, 510711

SWEDEN – SUÈDE
CE Fritzes AB
S–106 47 Stockholm   Tel. (08) 690.90.90
Telefax: (08) 20.50.21

Subscription Agency/Agence d'abonnements :
Wennergren-Williams Info AB
P.O. Box 1305
171 25 Solna   Tel. (08) 705.97.50
Telefax: (08) 27.00.71

SWITZERLAND – SUISSE
Maditec S.A. (Books and Periodicals - Livres
et périodiques)
Chemin des Palettes 4
Case postale 266
1020 Renens VD 1   Tel. (021) 635.08.65
Telefax: (021) 635.07.80

Librairie Payot S.A.
4, place Pépinet
CP 3212
1002 Lausanne   Tel. (021) 320.25.11
Telefax: (021) 320.25.14

Librairie Unilivres
6, rue de Candolle
1205 Genève   Tel. (022) 320.26.23
Telefax: (022) 329.73.18

Subscription Agency/Agence d'abonnements :
Dynapresse Marketing S.A.
38 avenue Vibert
1227 Carouge   Tel. (022) 308.07.89
Telefax: (022) 308.07.99

See also – Voir aussi :
OECD Publications and Information Centre
August-Bebel-Allee 6
D-53175 Bonn (Germany)   Tel. (0228) 959.120
Telefax: (0228) 959.12.17

THAILAND – THAÏLANDE
Suksit Siam Co. Ltd.
113, 115 Fuang Nakhon Rd.
Opp. Wat Rajbopith
Bangkok 10200   Tel. (662) 225.9531/2
Telefax: (662) 222.5188

TUNISIA – TUNISIE
Grande Librairie Spécialisée
Fendri Ali
Avenue Haffouz Imm El-Intilaka
Bloc B 1 Sfax 3000   Tel. (216-4) 296 855
Telefax: (216-4) 298.270

TURKEY – TURQUIE
Kültür Yayinlari Is-Türk Ltd. Sti.
Atatürk Bulvari No. 191/Kat 13
Kavaklidere/Ankara
    Tel. (312) 428.11.40 Ext. 2458
Telefax: (312) 417 24 90
Dolmabahce Cad. No. 29
Besiktas/Istanbul   Tel. (212) 260 7188

UNITED KINGDOM – ROYAUME-UNI
HMSO
Gen. enquiries   Tel. (171) 873 8242
Postal orders only:
P.O. Box 276, London SW8 5DT
Personal Callers HMSO Bookshop
49 High Holborn, London WC1V 6HB
Telefax: (171) 873 8416
Branches at: Belfast, Birmingham, Bristol,
Edinburgh, Manchester

UNITED STATES – ÉTATS-UNIS
OECD Publications and Information Center
2001 L Street N.W., Suite 650
Washington, D.C. 20036-4922 Tel. (202) 785.6323
Telefax: (202) 785.0350

Subscriptions to OECD periodicals may also be placed through main subscription agencies.

Les abonnements aux publications périodiques de l'OCDE peuvent être souscrits auprès des principales agences d'abonnement.

Orders and inquiries from countries where Distributors have not yet been appointed should be sent to: OECD Publications Service, 2, rue André-Pascal, 75775 Paris Cedex 16, France.

Les commandes provenant de pays où l'OCDE n'a pas encore désigné de distributeur peuvent être adressées à : OCDE, Service des Publications, 2, rue André-Pascal, 75775 Paris Cedex 16, France.

1-1996

OECD PUBLICATIONS, 2, rue André-Pascal, 75775 PARIS CEDEX 16
PRINTED IN FRANCE
(66 96 05 1) ISBN 92-64-14795-0 – No. 48609 1996